Courage: Daring Poems for Gutsy Girls

❧

Edited by Karen Finneyfrock,
Rachel McKibbens,
and Mindy Nettifee

Write Bloody Publishing
America's Independent Press

Austin, TX

WRITEBLOODY.COM

Courage: Daring Poems for Gutsy Girls

© 2014 Write Bloody Publishing
No part of this book may be used or performed without written consent from the author, except for critical articles or reviews.

Write Bloody
First Edition
ISBN: 978-1938912207

Cover art by Lily Lin
Proofread by Mindy Nettifee
Edited by Karen Finneyfrock, Mindy Nettifee, and Rachel McKibbens
Interior layout by Ashley Siebels

Type set in Bergamo from www.theleagueofmoveabletype.com

Printed in Tennessee, USA

Write Bloody Publishing
Austin, TX
Support Independent Presses
writebloody.com

To contact the author, send an email to writebloody@gmail.com

MADE IN THE USA

COURAGE: DARING POEMS FOR GUTSY GIRLS

Courage: Daring Poems For Gutsy Girls

FOR TEETH
ON POWER AND PROTECTION

HOW TO EAT SUGARCANE
ON LOVE AND LOSS

FROM THE ECHO CHAMBER
ON BEING AND BECOMING

BLOODLINE
ON FAMILY AND FAITH

MIRROR ANTHEMS
ON ESTEEM AND EXPOSURE

The Wild Language of Stars
On Healing and Living

Courage is a daughter's name.

— NIKKY FINNEY

Introduction

Maybe you were a teenage girl once. Maybe you are a teenage girl right now. And maybe you know and love a teenage girl, or someone who was once. If you have picked up this book, you know that teenage-girlhood is special territory, the metaphorical dark woods through which every girl must walk. There are the facts of it, sure – hormones, highschool, bestfriends, crushes, cars; all the dreaded pressures and anticipated firsts. But it is also a time of great mystery, and magic, and initiation. A time of choosing where and how to go, and becoming who you're going to become; a time of facing harrowing obstacles and great change.

In other words: totally overwhelming.

We can't control the world teenage girls will inhabit and participate in creating. But if we could give them one charm to tuck into their pockets, it would be courage. So, in lieu of a sword, or a yellow brick road, here is a book. In it we have packed poems to shock you, and make you laugh, poems that will commiserate and grieve with you; poems that will inspire you, and give you what you need to face life with grace and guts. These are the poems we wish we had had when we were younger.

They're not all easy or "classroom friendly." And not every topic is covered and not every voice represented because one book can't contain it all. We selected each one for inspiring courage through voice. In this anthology there are mothers and daughters and cackling sisters; there are spells, warnings, myths, and knowing glances. This is a gathering of some of the most captivating voices in contemporary poetry today. You are going to come out of this party with at least three favorite poems. Pinky swear.

The Editors

Karen, Rachel and Mindy

MADE OF LIGHTNING

ESTEPHANIA
By Cristin O'Keefe Aptowicz

Maybe it was my habitually dirty mouth,
or my habitually dirty hair, or maybe it was
the way cockiness and bragging would prop
their charcoal feet on my irises, mindlessly

stoking the haughty fire of my tongue.
Maybe it was my childhood's lack of ribbons
and Barbies, my zeal at being the only kid
ghoulish enough to slice meaty nightcrawlers
with my thumbnail for perching on dad's hook,
but whatever it was, I saw myself as a boy's girl.

I didn't know what to do with myself when
visiting with female friends: their canopy beds,
their ceramic harlequin masks, their photo albums
made of puffy fabric and glitter paint. Their mothers
sensed my wildness, nervously handing me

tumblers of iced tea destined to be knocked over,
the relentless jitter of limbs, my dirty nails,
the unforgivably sorry mess of me. In the fifth grade,
we met: two pudgy collections of fashion mistakes,
two braying sacks of girl giggles and buck teeth,

and God gave you the impossible task of guiding
me through to womanhood, our friendship tugging me
together when my mouth exploded all over itself,
the gentle counsel of your eyes, the generous salve
of your laugh, the unintentional comedy of our hair.

Our teen years read like a satire on unloveablity,
our diaries like racing forms just trying to keep up
with the latest of our galloping, resistible hearts.
There were years when we were never kissed,
there were boys who'd threatened the tender

sinews of our shared self, times we wanted
to shatter the mirror of each other's bodies:
I am not you! I could never ever be you!
and yet here we are. Almost twenty years later:
full grown and fleshed out, with love finally

sleeping sweetly in our own beds. On Sunday,
we shared perhaps our millionth meal, banging
our laughs together like ceremonial gongs, and
I marveled at the startling women who sprouted
from such riotous, unstoppable and perfect girls.

★From *Oh, Terrible Youth*

SHOULDA BEEN JIMI SAVANNAH
By Patricia Smith

My mother scraped the name Patricia Ann from the ruins
of her discarded Delta, thinking it would offer me shield
and shelter, that leering men would skulk away at the slap
of it. Her hands on the hips of Alabama, she went for flat
and functional, then siphoned each syllable of drama,
repeatedly crushing it with her broad, practical tongue
until it sounded like an instruction to God and not a name.
She wanted a child of pressed head and knocking knees,
a trip-up in the doubledutch swing, a starched pinafore
and peppermint-in-the-sour pickle kinda child, stiff-laced
and unshakably fixed on salvation. *Her* Patricia Ann
would never idly throat the Lord's name or wear one
of those thin, sparkled skirts that flirted with her knees.
She'd be a nurse or a third-grade teacher or a postal drone,
jobs requiring alarm clock discipline and sensible shoes.
My four downbeats were music enough for a vapid life
of butcher shop sawdust and fatback as cuisine, for Raid
spritzed into the writhing pockets of a Murphy bed.
No crinkled consonants or muted hiss would summon me.

My daddy detested borders. One look at my mother's
watery belly, and he insisted, as much as he could insist
with her, on the name Jimi Savannah, seeking to bless me
with the blues-bathed moniker of a ball breaker, the name
of a grown gal in a snug red sheath and unlaced All-Stars.
He wanted to shoot muscle through whatever I was called,
arm each syllable with tiny weaponry so no one would
mistake me for anything other than a tricky whisperer
with a switchblade in my shoe. I was bound to be all legs,
a bladed debutante hooked on Lucky Strikes and sugar.
When I sent up prayers, God's boy would giggle and consider.

Daddy didn't want me to be anybody's sure-fire factory,
nobody's callback or seized rhythm, so he conjured
a name so odd and hot even a boy could claim it. And yes,

he was prepared for the look my mother gave him when
he first mouthed his choice, the look that said, *That's it,
you done lost your goddamned mind.* She did that thing
she does where she grows two full inches with righteous,
and he decided to just whisper *Love you, Jimi Savannah*
whenever we were alone, re- and rechristening me the seed
of Otis, conjuring his own religion and naming it me.

*From *Shoulda Been Jimi Savannah*

When Tip Drill Comes on at the Frat Party Or, When Refusing to Twerk Is a Radical Form of Self-Love

By Fatimah Asghar

After Danez

Sometimes it's as simple as the reminder of numbers
& ridged plastic sliding through an ass: bent, shaking,
whirring up like an arcade game when touched.

Sometimes it's as simple as the boys, howling
under bright lights, who only see the dissected
parts of you—
      nose, wrist, nape of neck, nipple—

that which can be held down, pinned back, cut open,
frog heart pounding & exposed to the science class
of club & white boy & hands.

Sometimes it's as simple as sweaty nails pushing
gritty into your stomach, the weight of claws ripping
at the button on your jeans.

Sometimes it's as simple as a look from your best friend,
alive on the dance floor, the light of her own sweet sweat
to realize the powerhouse in you, to realize the sum

of your body, not its dissected parts but the whole,
damn, breathing thing. Sometimes it's as simple
as standing still amid all the moving & heat & card

& plastic & science & sway & say:
                No.
                Today, this body,
                is mine.

I SING THE BODY ELECTRIC, ESPECIALLY WHEN MY POWER'S OUT

By Andrea Gibson

This is my body
I have weather veins.
They are especially sensitive
to dust storms and hurricanes.
When I am nervous my teeth chatter
like a wheelbarrow collecting rain.
I am rusty when I talk.
It's the storm in me.

The doctor says someday
I might not be able to walk.
It's in my blood like the iron.
My mother is tough as nails.
She held herself together
the day she could no longer hold my niece
she said, "Our knee caps are our prayer beds.
Everyone can walk further on their kneecaps
than they can on their feet."

This is my heartbeat.
Like yours, it is a hatchet.
It can build a house
or tear one down.

My mouth is a fire escape.
The words coming out can't care that they are naked.
There is something burning in here.
When it burns I hold my own shell to my ear,
listen for the parade when I was seven
the man who played the bagpipes
wore a skirt.
He was from Scotland so
I wanted to move there,
wanted my spine to be the spine

of an unpublished book
my faith the first and last page.

The day my ribcage becomes monkey bars
for a girl hanging on my every word

they said "You are not allowed to love her."
Tried to take me by the throat
to teach me I was not a boy.

I had to unlearn their prison speak,
refused to make wishes on the star
on the sheriff's chest.

I started wishing on the stars instead.
I said to the sun, "Tell me about the big bang."
The sun said, "It hurts to become."

I carry that hurt on the tip of my tongue
and whisper "bless your heart" every chance I get
so my family tree can be sure I have not left.

You do not have to leave to arrive.
I am learning this slowly.
So sometimes when I look in the mirror
my eyes look like the holes in the shoes
of the shoe shine man.

Sometimes my hands are busy on the wrong things.
Some days I call my arms "wings"
while my head is in clouds.

It will take me a few more years to learn flying
is not pushing away the ground.

But safety isn't always safe.
You can find one on every gun.
I am aiming to do better.
This is my body.

My exhaustion pipe will never pass inspection
and still my lungs know how to breathe
like a burning map
every time I get lost in the curtain of her hair,
you can find me by the window
following my past
to that trail of blood in the snow.

The night I opened my veins
the doctor who stitched me up
asked me if I did it for attention.

For the record, if you have ever done anything for attention
this poem is attention.
Title it with your name.
It will pace the city bridge every night
you stand staring at the river.
It never wants to find your body
doing anything but loving what it loves.

Love what you love
Say, "This is my body
It is no one's but mine."
This is my nervous system,
my wanting blood,
my half tamed addictions,
my tongue tied up
like a ball of Christmas lights.

if you put a star on the top of my tree
make sure it's a star that fell,
make sure it hit bottom
like a tambourine
'cause all these words are stories for the staircase
to the top of lungs
where I sing what hurts
and the echo comes back saying
"Bless your heart.
Bless your holy kneecaps,

they are so smart.
You are so full of rain.
There is so much that's growing.
Hallelujah to your weather veins.
Hallelujah to the ache, to the pull
to the fall, to the pain.
Hallelujah to the grace in the body
In every cell of us all.

★From *The Madness Vase*

Black Girl From Beverly Encounters the Messy Bun

By Jamila Woods

O sloppy tangle of dirty blonde hairs.
Windswept bundle bound by Walgreen's elastic.
Your scrunchie runneth over. A bouquet
of bone straight strands, haphazardly gathered
smelling of shampoo and eau de Catholic school girl.

My middle school aspiration to sculpt
a replica of your asymmetrical blossom
with my stubborn plot of brittle grass
was destined to fail.

Still, each morning I rolled a bale of Black
hay up the nape of my neck. A Sisyphus stone
of stiff dark strands forever refusing to submit
to rubber band or gravity.

The Last Spell of the Sea Witch

By Karen Finneyfrock

"But a mermaid has no tears, and therefore she suffers so much more."
—Hans Christian Andersen

I only need to stand near a bowl of water, or by a half-full
shaker of salt, to offer you the north wind in a rope knotted
or a ship with a pregnant sail. Given a conch shell filled
with driftwood and enough seaweed to strangle a mare,
I could load your deck with gasping tuna, shoo barnacles
from the hull like I'm sweeping the floor. But I'll need a shipwreck
to offer you true love or legs or whatever the girls beg me for this time.

Give us perfect breasts, they tell me, *and eyes the color
of snake oil. Give us hips that fit into vinyl dresses. Give
us claws to keep the men we beckon.* Does anyone wish
for Heaven anymore? Once girls wanted eternity, a soul
to barter with and a kingdom above the spray. Now
they ask for flawless photographs, armies demanding
their signature, songs written in the key of them.

I am a dying sea witch, scaly with kelp and pruned, I won't leave
you moaning *girls should be different.* Girls will live in the world
as they make it. But think of me. When you stand by the boat's rail
and the wind pulls pins from your hair. Old women were girls once,
testing their voices on the men who sailed past them. Sometimes
the prince doesn't love you. Don't put all your hope on legs.

PRIVATE PARTS

By Sarah Kay

The first love of my life never saw me naked.
There was always a parent coming home in a half hour,
always a little brother in the next room, always too much
body and not enough time for me to show him.

Instead, I gave him a shoulder, an elbow, the bend
of my knee. I lent him my corners, my edges:
the parts of me I could afford to offer, the parts of me
I had long since given up trying to hide.

He never asked for more. He gave me back his eyelashes,
the back of his neck, his palms. We held every piece we were given
like it was a nectarine—might bruise if we weren't careful—
we collected them like we were trying to build an orchard.

And the spaces that he never saw: the ones my parents
had labeled "Private Parts" when I was still small enough
to fit all of my self and worries inside a bathtub,
I made up for them by handing over all the private parts of me.

There was no secret I did not tell him,
there was no moment we did not share.
We didn't grow up, we grew in: like ivy wrapping,
molding each other into perfect yings and yangs.

We kissed with mouths open, breathing his exhale
into my inhale and back. We could have survived
underwater or in outer space, living only off the breath
we traded. We spelled "love" G-I-V-E.

I never wanted to keep my body from him.
If I could have, I am sure I would have given it all away
with the rest of me. I did not know it was possible
to keep some things for myself.

Some nights, I wake up knowing he is anxious.
He is across the world in another woman's arms
and the years have spread us like dandelion seeds,
sanding down the edges of our jigsaw parts that used to only fit each other.

He drinks from the pitcher on the night stand, checks
the digital clock, it is five am. He tosses in sheets and
tries to settle. I wait for him to sleep, before tucking myself
into elbows and knees; reaching for things I have long since given away.

ON A MISSION TRIP TO PHILADELPHIA
I BEGIN TO FEAR THE INSIDE OF MY BODY

By Traci Brimhall

In a tent we sing and lift our palms
    to the darkening sky. And I know it's a secret
        that all my prayers sound like questions.

And it's a secret that a boy touches
    my shins when no one is looking.
        but my brother or sister died inside her,

and I've tried to picture this as two of me
    My mother once told me I was a twin,
        in one bed. When I cover my eyes and count

three—two—one—the other is gone.
    I used to think my body was made
        of bones and roses. How else to explain

the soul? Unpeel the layered corolla
and there's something waiting for wind
to release it. In school, we spread a map

of the circulatory system on the ground
    and took turns walking through it, explaining
        to our teacher *atrium—ventricle—aorta.*

And I went home and wept because my heart
    was no longer a mystery. This thing stirring
        in me was rhythmic, vascular. What if the world

can explain everything? Like why I dream
    of drowning children and wake up with wet hair.
        Or why, when the boy gives me oranges,
the fruit in his hand blushes. Or why, when my father
    can't clip his canaries' wings, he blinds them.
        And I wake up in darkness and know God loves me

with that kind of violence. The boy next to me stares
at my shins. The pastor's hand trembles over us.
I taste blood in my mouth, and it isn't mine.

13

By Aracelis Girmay

Eared, peacock,
silver-toothed body of arms,

10 toes, crooked hip,
farm of cartilage,
eyebrows cawing high
above red uterus collecting.

Follow down there,
down to that apple, then,
that female planet, viscous pomegranate
shade untouched by hands.

When you are root & wide enough one day,
you open your legs & see
that you have turned into a thin, blood silk,
fire shining red from the vagina,

13,
blessed,
all dragon.

*From *Teeth*

The Hurricane Sermons

AMETHYST ROCKSTAR

By Sara Brickman

One a.m. on a Saturday
and my parents will not let me go to Detroit
EVER AGAIN.
My father has waited up for me with disappointed eyes,
a police line on his tongue.

This is before cell phones,
when I carry quarters in my pocket
like miniature silver heavens,
the release of youth
a mere payphone away. But for once,
I have forgotten to call.

Have been up late
in a city whose hugeness calls to me like novels,
whose blackness quakes my parents from their sleep.
I have been out with queers,
poets and girls, the sweat of the outdoor
combination Saul Williams/techno concert dripping off of us
like hellfire, the rain drenching our tiny bodies.

I am glad for the wool socks that Sailor loaned me
before we ran to the van, before Boca the dog
licked my feet, and there were vegan sandwiches.
Bars that served 'til one a.m. Diners. A whole city
that is *really* a city, is really
an escape route, 20 minutes from the forest and dirt roads.
Where cramming into the van
I become a girl with teeth
and songs. A hollering sidewalk-walker with pit-bulls in her fists,
where I am not trying to decide who or what
I am in this body any longer,
but am the hand rocking my life
into its awakening. My father

and I stare at each other across the living room.
His joy that I have finally found friends
battling the beer on my breath.
His robe is a weapon that says, *I wrap myself in family.*
I am wrapped in the new raincoat my mother bought me,
but I am also wearing my new raincoat's first
cigarette burn. I reek of smoke. I wrap myself

in the silence of *daughter.*
It is when I first know what I belong to.
And what I will leave behind to get there.

7 Things I Never Told My Older Sister, Because I know Better, In Reverse Chronological Order

By Mindy Nettifee

1. If you ever feel like leaving him, renting a rich blue convertible and becoming someone else somewhere in the desert, I'll go with you.

2. Thank you for all the horrible and/or dangerous things you did first, so I could learn from your mistakes. Specifically: getting herpes, dropping out of school, getting a trendy dream catcher tattoo.

3. I dropped acid with your ex-girlfriend.

4. Back during your chunky crystals and channeling spirits phase, when you told me in the back seat of a Ford Taurus that you had spoken with my higher self and she was "really worried about me"? I haven't trusted myself since.

5. I took French in school because you did, and I thought we would be able to have top secret conversations about sex and drugs and rated R films in front of mom. Why didn't we do that?

6. I was the one that destroyed your Black Crowes tape, not the dog.

7. Every time you ran away from home, I followed you.

★From *Sleepyhead Assassins*

Synonyms For Courage (In the Key of Bipolar)

By Shira Erlichman

Bull-gouging-the-matador.
Dead snakecharmer.
Chef-with-no-hands.
Pacifist bullet.

Skinned. Poise.
Tunnelheat. Quiet. Dark.
Try. Hands. Girl.

Marathoner. Push.
Flower. Universal
push. Stay. Postpartum
whatever-it-takes.
Stay. Elegance.
Stillness. No.
Absolutely No.
Yes. Pills. Cool.
Brass. Kindness.
Weakness. Sky.

Limits. Try.
Try. Try. Art.
Hellgospel.
Spitsauce. Skirtpeace.
Monkhands.
Melted shoulders.
Walking.
Hunger. Stay. Weep. Mirror
polish.

Crawl. Hellelujah.
Unfold. Unflinch.
Underbelly.

Naked.
Neverdone.
Amen.

Opening night.
Truth-or-truth.

Rise.

LOVE THY NEIGHBOR

By Gypsee Yo (Jonida Beqo)

Brass knuckle Amnon and crooked jaw Cain
were Irish twins, fifteen and sixteen years old,
the spitting image of their mamma—a young,
black widow, a venom sharpshooter,
a thirty year drought.

They were my neighbors. We lived
on the third floor of the same concrete building.

Our doors stood at a perpetual face-off,
Cain's bed and mine barely separated
by a thin wall he often bruised with my name
punching through his teeth as he abused
himself. It was a sound so wretched,
no screaming radio could drown it out.

Cain was a shifting shadow with a vice grip
heart, squeezing life out of anything he loved.

His favorite game was to press a bird
between brick wall and jaw until he heard
its lungs crack like glass. He stuck bloody
feathers from his fresh kills under my door
like love letters.

He wrote me so many love letters,
made sure I found them everywhere:

Ribbons snatched from my shy hair
stuffed inside my slashed bicycle tires.
Guillotined butterflies in my shutters.
A rabbit's head thrust in the threshold.

Once he climbed the rain gutter, the lightning
of a dry storm, and pushed my only dress to suicide,
plunging it wet with fear from the third floor clothesline
down into the dusty courtyard. When I asked, in tears,
why he would do such a thing, he sneered,

"I just like to picture your body going down with it"

He only knew how to love a thing
when it was dead like a father.

Amnon was a mute mountain of mean
with hands twice the size of his body,
brass knuckle snares that once caught me
in the no-man's-land between our doors.

He pressed a nine millimeters' tongue
to the nape of my neck, and tightened
his left hand around my green plum chest.

I had better sense than to fight him.
I fixed my eyes on a curious crack in the wall
that inched closer to the pale ceiling each time
Cain banged his head against it on the other side,
a weeping captive of his brother's mockery.

It made me feel less alone to know
Amnon was torturing us both.

The day war broke out, men and boys
in the neighborhood rushed to kidnap guns
and rifles, fevered by that wicked spring.

Brass-Knuckle Amnon and Crooked-Jaw Cain
rode through the ruins on a stolen army tank
like serial killer cowboys, high on blood lust
and sniffed glue. They played marksman's
games with my humble window for days.

I survived those boys by the grace of God,
with a King James Bible and an old typewriter.

I punched keys with crooked jaws
to the rhythm of their weapons,
writing poems about love, forgiveness,
and things too much alive to die at their hands.

I fortified the wall between Cain's bed and mine
with pages from the book of Psalms.

"Great peace have them which love thy law,
and nothing shall offend them".

The day I left for America, Cain shot
every single flower pot still perched
on a window ledge in the neighborhood,
howling like a betrayed wolf.

I did not turn around to look at him.
I wished them both dead.

Years later, when word of their simultaneous deaths
reached me on a stifling hot Southern afternoon,
I went running in the backwoods, the son in my womb
churning as I wept ferociously for them:

The bonfire bones of the men they were ripened
into, and the shrapnel of the boys beneath.

Before brass knuckles and crooked jaws,
before their bodies ignited inside a melting car
at the scene of a common drug bust in Sicily
they were two naked infants on a cold tile floor,
begging with chilling shrills for the breasts
of a mother shrouded in death and anger.

How she concealed milk and love beneath a heavy,
black dress, locked fanatically by a long line of bone
buttons, running from her venomous throat all the way
down to her bare feet. How she poisoned them slowly
to avenge her solitude. How they loved me, mean
like a mother.

"For as a man hath destroyed his enemy;
so hast thou lost the love of thy neighbor."

A Letter to the Playground Bully, From Andrea, Age 8 ½

By Andrea Gibson

Maybe there are cartwheels in your mouth.
Maybe your words will grow up to be gymnasts.
Maybe you have been kicking people with them by accident.

I know some people get a whole lot of rocking
in the rocking chair
and the ones who don't
sometimes get rocks in their voice boxes
and their voice boxes become slingshots.

Maybe you think my heart
looks like a baby squirrel.
But you absolutely missed
when you told the class I have head lice
because I one hundred percent absolutely
do not have head lice
and even if I do
it's a fact that head lice prefer clean heads over dirty ones
so I am clean as a whistle on a teapot.

My mother says it is totally fine
if I blow off steam
as long as I speak in an octave
my kindness can still reach.

My kindness knows mermaids
never ever miss their legs in the water
'cause there are better ways to move
through an ocean than kicking.

So guess what, if I ever have my own team
I am picking everyone first,
even the worst kid
and the kid with the stutter
like a skipping record

because I know all of us are scratched,
even if you can't hear it when we speak.

My mother says some people have heartbeats
that are knocking on doors that will never open,
and I know my heart is a broken freezer chest,
that's why I can't keep anything frozen,
so no, I am not "always crying."
I am just thawing outside of the lines.

And even if I am "always crying"
it is a fact that salt is the only reason
everything floats so good in the Dead Sea.

And just 'cause no one ever passes notes to me
doesn't mean I am not super duper.
In fact, my super duper might be a buoy or a paper boat
the next time your nose gets stuck up the river
because it is a fact

that our hearts stop every time we sneeze
and some people's houses have too much dust.

Some people's fathers are like addicts.
I've heard attics have monsters in their walls
and shaky stares.
I lived in a house with attic
I think I'd nightmare a burglar in my safety chest,
and maybe I'd look for rest
in the sticks and stones
because my mother says
a kid can only swallow so much punch
before he's drunk on his own fist.

But the only drunk I have ever known
was sleeping in the alley behind my church
and Jesus turned water into his wine
so even god has his bad days.

But on your bad days couldn't you just say,
"I'm having a bad day,"
instead of telling me I'm stupid or poor
or telling me I dress like a boy
because maybe I am a boy and a girl,

maybe my name is Andrea-Andrew, so what?
It is a fact that bumblebees have hair on their eyeballs
and people, also, should comb
through everything they see.

For instance, an anchorman is not a sailor,
and the clouds might be a pillow fight.

My mother says,
"Every bird perched on a telephone wire
will listen to the conversations running through its' feet
to decide the direction of its flight,"
so I know every word we speak
can make hurricanes in peoples' weather veins
or shine their shiny shine.

So maybe sometime if somebody
would sit beside me on the bus
I could say, "Guess what, it is a fact
that manatees have vocal chords
even though they don't have ears,
and Beethoven made music
even when he could no longer hear,

and I know every belt that has hit someone's back
is still a belt that was built to hold something up."

And it is fact that Egyptians slept on pillows made of stone
but it's not hard for me to dream
that maybe one day you'll write me back
like the day I wrote the lightening bug to say,
"I smashed my mason jar and I threw away the lid."

I didn't want to take a chance that I'd grow up to be a war.
I want to be a belly dance, or an accordion, or a pogo stick
or the fingerprints the mason left
in the mortar between the bricks
to prove that he was here,

that he built a roof over someone's head
to keep the storm from their faith.
My mother says that's why we all were born.

And I think she's right.
So write back soon.
Sincerely yours.

*From *The Madness Vase*

THE THING I SAID THAT DURING GYM

By Shaney Jean Maney

made that kid's face break, and I knew I ruined his everything.

There are times when you can see words
burst from your mouth. When you wanna reach out and
catch them with your hands, crumple them up, burn them.

The thing wasn't clever or true. It wasn't smart.
It was terrible. Nonchalant. A thing someone else's
dad would say, then laugh.

Before I spoke, they had been talking about me.
The way I seemed too friendly with other girls.
My socks. My laugh. My braces. How queer I seemed.

I think his name was Joey. First, Joey accidentally
hearing. Then, what disbelief and shock and pain look like
when they are added up on Joey's unsuspecting face.

The awful pile of throat lump I kept for the day,
for the month. The guilty lump that twenty years later
wrote this poem.

I could never take it back. I could never take it back.
I could never take it back.

THELMA TODD

By Amber Tamblyn

This Svedka-sponsored T-Mobile party
tucked into the tight shoulder blades of the Pacific Palisades
is honoring the lifetime achievements of Christina Aguilera.

In the background Debbie Harry croons
for a terrace of people titillated
only for their text messages.

I'm in some dark hallway, cornered
by an actress in a bandage dress,
burned one too many times,
whose cocktail is doing all the healing,

sloshing on about the good ol' days,
back when we were all periodless and vivacious,
our winning auditions clinging to our underwear.

How we'd piss victory,
brush the rejection from our hair.

She wants to know what I think of Annie—
how vulgar her success is,
what a tragedy it's all become,
am I also allergic to her over-annunciations?

She wants to know if I've heard
about the role opposite the handsome future failure,
am I getting in line
to lose weight for the seventh-chance director.

Do I want advice, in general, but more specifically,
on how to blow up my breasts
into fame balloons,
send them up to the helium angels
on a string body?

Your career has another 5 years, maybe, she says, *if you're lucky.*
According to who? I ask.
According to every actress who's come before you.

So I turn my focus to every actress
coming after me.

I wade through the crowd with a canister of judgment,
tag the trains of every dress, leave my mark on their scars.

At the bar I run into Nancy,
drinking away her forties,
her eyes flush broken compasses.
Lost between age fifteen and fifty.

Fermented blood.
Deep sea drinker.

I do not look into her ocean.
The fish there float to the bottom.
I fear I'll go down there too,
identifying with the abyss.
Washed up.
Banging on the backdoor of a black hole.

I plow through the women's room doors
into cool tiled silence.
Run warm water over my shaking hands.
Above the sink, above the mirror,
a picture of the bar's first owner stares down at me,

that Dust Bowl Era actress
who killed herself in that Lincoln
or fell asleep with the engine running.
Maybe it was a Packard Convertible.

She would've had to make her comeback too.

When the coroner cut her open, he found only
peas and beans in her stomach. No blue moonstones
beneath old-fashioned bandages.

I look down at the sink, the water brimming over
the top of my wrists and onto the floor.
I do not tell my fingers what to do.
My hands are not my hands. They are the water
surrounded by swirling, singing, overflowing stars.

FOREST FIRES

By Sarah Kay

I arrive home from JFK in the rosy
hours to find a new 5-in-1 egg slicer
and dicer on our dining room table.
This is how my father deals with grief.

Three days ago, I was in the Santa Cruz
Redwoods tracing a mountain road
in the back of a pickup truck, watching
clouds unravel into spider webs.

Two days from now, there will be
forest fires, so thick, they will have to
evacuate Santa Cruz. The flames will paint
the Evening News a different shade of orange,

and when it happens, I will be in New York City
watching something else on TV. Commercials,
probably, which is all that seems to play
on hospital television sets: the beeping

from the nurses' station mixing with sales jingles—
the theme song for the ailing. My grandmother's tiny body
is a sinking ship on white sheets. I hold her hand
and try to remember open highway.

It really goes to show that it doesn't take
much with these dry conditions to start a fire,
a CalFire spokesman will tell CNN on Sunday.
Fire officials have been working tirelessly, but

controlling something this big is impossible.
My mother will point at the celluloid flames,
remind me how lucky I am, how close I had been,
how narrowly I missed this disaster. My father

will point out a commercial for the Brown N' Crisp,
repeat line by line how it bakes, broils, steams,
fries and barbeques. He will write down
the number to order it later.

Three days ago, I was barefoot. Balancing
on train tracks, the full moon an unexpected visitor,
the smoke-free air as clean and sharp
as these city lungs could stand.

Two days from now I will find my father
making egg salad in the kitchen, exhausted
after an all-night shift at the hospital. I will
ask if he needs help and understand

when he says no, I will leave him to slice
and dice the things he can. My grandmother
folds her hands on mine and strokes
my knuckles like they are a wild animal she is

trying to tame. She tells me I am gorgeous,
watches a commercial, forgets my name,
tells me I am gorgeous again.
My father watches from the bedside chair,

his mother and daughter strung together
with tightrope hands, fingers that look
like his own. And somewhere in California
a place I once stood is burning.

FOR TEETH

Una Oración

By Rachel McKibbens

(where I explain the origins of my appetite for destruction)

I arrived one body part at a time. First the scalloped middle,
blue-roped torso. Eyes, nose & ears, bloodlicked.
Then the blur of this electric mouth, the wet unfolding
of my arms, legs, and fists. The last, of course, this cauldron
of a cunt. The nurses delivered me to my parents
on a dinner plate. Father howled. Mother thinned down
to a milkless shadow. I have always been a god-hammered girl.
Dirty as a turnip, I crawled into the blind center of the earth.
A worm built to outlast the swallow. Listen. Anything holy
is not reversible. There isn't a man alive who could undo me.

JESSICA

By Gypsee Yo (Jonida Beqo)

When she was born a girl,
her father picked up the axe
and tore down the stillhouse
bit by bit, till the sluggish air clotted
with the blood of moonshine.

He worked on cars until his hands fell out
through the warped mouth of the pickup
window, yawning with him, asleep
at the wheel in the greatest pile of wreckage
anyone ever saw this side of Highway 31.

Her mother ran her own elbows
through the kitchen blades again
and again until shreds of her name
snowed all over the trailer park
like a cautionary folk tale.

The first time a boy dared
to lift the meridian of her skirt,
Jesse slapped him so hard,
he saw freckles in the sky.

"You better meet me
by the flagpole."

she said, barging through
the school's double doors,
fists full of his fat angel curls.

His boyhood challenged,
he was dumb enough to show
up under the stars and stripes,
where she mashed his pretty cheeks
like new taters on a hungry table.

*"Mah daddy said, if you'd like
to keep yer hands, best
keep them to yerself!"*

Some girls sleep dormant in the red dirt,
the heavy fruit of their too-soon children
withering the roots of youthful dreams.

They take to the bottle,
they take to the gossip,
they take to the whip
to shake off the despair.

Some girls line up in perfect rules:
in rows, and pews, and cubical days
inching away in the tunnel of time
afraid of the spark, the light, the danger.

They take to the closet, they take to the scale,
they take to rustle of magazine pages
to drown out the voice beneath their doctored skin.

But some girls unfurl against the sky,
muster the courage for the take off
out of the worst wreckage seen
this side of the blue.

They take to the air
like they were born for it.

They stretch their hands outside
the window of the life they were given
and grab a new one by the mane.

THE FIRST TIME I HIT A BOY

By Mindy Nettifee

It doesn't matter that I smile too big and too much,
or that my looks shout warning like a poodle shouts guard dog:
he was dumb enough to say cruel things about my sister
to my face. *Hey, how come you turned out so pretty*
and she turned out so butt ugly? and then POP! KABLAM!
or, you know, however the comic book boys would say it—
I swung. Hard. And did not miss.

There's not much else to the story.
I'd never met my fist, and then I did.
I was twelve.
I had barely tasted anger.
It was like a mouth full of copper pennies.
Hate wishes.

The other kids just froze there in circle around us,
their mouths opening on their hinges then rusting there.
It hurt like hell when his braces grated my knuckles,
and we both cried out like girls, though he squeaked more
from trying to hold it in and looked genuinely hurt
when he asked *what did you do that for?*

I was speechless, because I knew, but I didn't know.
I was as surprised as he was
to find I had fuses, to discover them blown.
Everyone stared and stared for the longest time
and then a few of the other boys started to laugh,
doubled over even.
There was a trickle of coins on the sidewalk
and then, *then* he was changed forever.

Fury and pity flickered on and off in me.
This was also the first time I learned
there were a thousand strangers inside of me.
Some of them were violent.
The only one with an answer to his question
hadn't yet learned to speak.

MY GIRLS

By Hollis Wong-Wear

every night for three months
i dreamt about guns.
thick, sweltering
sawed off and anonymous
no matter where i was they found me/ shot me dead
until my alarm went off
and i woke up gasping
like morning was the afterlife
the dreams only stopped
when i stopped running
stared my fate in its barreled face
and got accustomed to the dark that followed

my girls and i,
we get accustomed to things
and in school
it's no fun to be the token feminist
and work is unbearable
if you're not cool with harassment
even though you know better
it is what it is
and you learn when to keep your mouth shut
even when you know it's wrong
so that things will just go by quicker

to be a girl means to flow with it
skin soft from being trapped in currents
to be a girl is to know
that life is suffering
and also first impressions
to bear weight
while constantly trying to lose it
to wear high heels
and lower your voice
to be a girl means

to say yes more often than not
because resistance is just more pressure
when you're an air chamber embodied
and us girls, we are our bodies
more than anything

and sometimes, we dream about guns
there is death in loaded things
and we know how intimate a gun can be
how a gun can smile and buy you a drink
or be your best friend, or say it loves you
a gun rarely catches you in the shadowed alleyway nowadays
but rather in your own bedroom
safety off, and we know
that guns fire for bad reasons
and for stupid reasons
and sometimes guns didn't mean it
but we also know how shrapnel stays
and we weren't born with weaponry
so we gotta be smart

but crossing your legs
doesn't spare you from the crossfire
and some of the smartest girls i know
become bodies in the moment
our voices go velvet
swallowed and stored
in the pink smallness of our throats
too afraid to pull the trigger of our tongue
our fingers in half-fist as
we grasp to catch what's shed
we allow those thresholds in our heads to give,
because our bodies were made to give
lines get crossed while we're
wondering where the poetry in all this is

but there are no pretty words
or bow-tied explanations
girls tongue the word rape
like a barb
that pierces us again and again
sometimes it hurts more
that that first time

it is much easier to think about guns
we dream about holding them in our
small hands, ones we can claim,
fantasize about the weight of them,
the cool steel, the small shells,
the death in them
call it penis envy
or call it any means necessary
even sorority girls know
that the system makes a victim suspect

you could have stopped it
and it's your fault, your fault
you are a girl, and you have a body
and you do not have a gun
but you have a fault,
seismic and unsolvable
a deep rift
for a gun to fit

us girls are expected
to smell like rosebuds
but more often we waft blood
my girls aren't flowers
my girls and I,
we're no metaphor
we are our bodies
soft, leathered and ours
who gotta be smart
and refuse to be a holster for
some man's gun.

SOUTH AMERICA ADDRESSES HER LATEST CONQUISTADOR

By April Ranger

*"So on our way to the party, Ben and I decided we'd name all the
pretty girls countries as they walked in, and then we'd like, claim
them, you know? Anyway, you came in and I was like, 'Damn.
That's South America. And she's mine."*

Good. I've always wanted to be a crumbling sheet of ice
at a shabby rink, waiting for the weight of a Zamboni
to drag over me and make me more suitable for blades.

I've always wanted to be called something I am not.
I have been unplowed land
growing fertile for the dig of your hands all these years.
I have been asleep in a tower ten decades.
Come! Drive your tongue between my lips
like a stake into parting soil,
parting is so easy,
my legs are designed this way,
they have hinges,
swinging doors between the kitchen and the dining room,
this is where the heat is,
I have prepared a feast
for you to take away.

I am a grape,
heavy on the vine,
hoping you will pluck me
and crush me into wine.

Since the word 'country'
apparently has ambiguous meaning to you,
call me country of the Moon,
mythologized for thousands of years,
just recently stepped upon.
Better yet, call me the country of the Sun, darling,
then climb your way to me.
The sun is so unmapped
and how do you relate to anything
if you haven't seen your own footprint in it?
Without you, I am merely babbling in my own language.
Teach me your speak, sir.

No, really.
I am in earnest now.
Dude.
Explain the word power to me.
Tell me why you feel so small.

POEM FOR REPELLING GHOSTS

By Karen Finneyfrock

Opposite each door, place a horseshoe. If not a horseshoe, then garlic.
No garlic? Recall garlic frying.

Wear jewelry made of wind chimes. Lanyard the doorknobs
in silver spoons. When the ghost comes stalking through your rosemary
garden say, "Don't come with those chains in your mouth to rattle
my gutters. Keep your unfinished business off my lawn."

Hang mirrors above the doors. Think positive
thoughts while wearing jewelry made of salt.

If the ghost comes back, yell, "I've got dynamite in my basement
and a restraining order reinstated." Pour graveyard dirt on his Sunday shirt.

Never try to harm the ghost or back him into a corner,
only say Go and mean that you mean it. Ghosts don't know
they're ghosts and never understand they're unwanted.

When your ghost leaves bleeding fog from beneath his sheet,
follow him to the traffic light with your eyes. Keep your feet
underneath you whatever you do. Lock the windows.

Make sure the neighbors see it all.

December

By Erica Miriam Fabri

There is a girl named December
who works as a hairdresser's assistant
on the Upper East Side. She wears black
lipstick, and has strong fingers. She gives
the best shampoo in all of Manhattan.

Middle-aged women love her, because
she doesn't make them feel awkward
about the tiny facelift scars that have formed
ridges around their ears. December lives
in a four-floor walkup, one-room apartment,
all by herself, except for her six-foot python.

As she massages avocado balm into the tender
scalps of New York City's fanciest ladies,
she tells them how her snake just turned
eight. She winks, like a loyal housewife,
when she says: "I've raised him since he was a born.
Eight whole years we've been together."

She explains to them, how she can't bear
to keep him in a tank, how he has the run
of their home, just like a dog would, and how
he sleeps in her bed each night,
in a tight coil at her ankles.

But lately, December sighs, "He's been acting strange.
He's refused to eat for weeks. He turns his head
in disinterest at the plump rats I bring him for dinner.
Pretends as if he cannot even smell their fur.

And the most unusual thing:
in the deepest part of night,
he unwinds his body and stretches out
alongside me in the bed,
as if he were a man."

She took him right away
to a Herp Vet out in Staten Island.
She had to take a boat to get there.
"And would you believe
what that fool for a snake doctor
tried to tell me?" December said.

"He said my snake has been starving himself,
to prepare for a big meal.
He said when he reaches his body long and straight,
to match the whole length of me on the mattress,
it's because he's measuring me.
He said he's planning to eat me.
That the only option is to put him to sleep immediately."

December wraps warm towels around
the necks of her clients as she tells them
this next part, the most important part, of the story.
"I looked straight at that doctor and said,
        Sir, you really think I would kill
        the very thing I love most?
        I know you are an expert in the workings
        of the internal organs of reptiles. But clearly,
        you know nothing about the heart of a woman."

She carried her snake all the way home,
from one island to another. He was heavier
than ever tonight. She carried him up
four flights of stairs. They fell asleep
right away, twisted together like ivy.

Back at the salon, the women waiting
to have their hair washed shook
their heads left and right in despair.
The eldest one said:
"December, you are young,
you have not yet learned
how love can ruin you.
You are so naïve,
you can't believe,
that the very thing
you sleep with
could swallow you."

SWARM

By Jeanann Verlee

Learn how to say "no."

Cram that word inside your mouth,
the whole thing, make sure all of it
gets in there. Let it walk on your tongue.
Practice with it in the mirror, push it
out, make faces, learn to love the salt
and bitter of it. Teach it to perch on your lip,
buzz, collect pollen from your sugary gloss.
Make it swarm between your cheeks.

Then, when the days come (there will be
many) where he pushes too hard, speaks
too sweetly, when the hand at your thigh
draws a thump in your stomach, when
the bitch gremlin inside whispers it's not
worth the fight, says you can barter
for your worth tomorrow, when your ribs
shrink, when he unfurls his Almighty Smile,
when four come at you at once, when
you love someone else, when the bar
is closing and your name becomes Take
What I Can Get, when the girls hate you
anyway, when you want him until the burn
if only he wore a different face—

pull back your lips, bare the teeth you have
sharpened to their perfect points, flick
your stinger tongue, set free your swarm.

*From Racing Hummingbirds

In Case You Ever Need It, It Is Here

By Daphne Gottlieb

Take this as yours
Rip this from the book
or make a copy
fold it in half
and half again
and put it in your wallet
or between the mattress and the box spring
or taped under your desk
so it is there
if.

Know this: what happened
to your body
to your head
to your heart
is not your fault.
It is not something you
deserved or caused.

It is like blaming yourself
for someone hitting your hand
with a hammer.
(if that person is you,
put the hammer down.
Let it be an accident.
Let it be the end.)

The body, heart, brain knows
how to heal. It knows how to knit
back together. How to suture
and secure. Let it do what it does.
Your body is yours. Your body
will always be yours.

You are not what happened.
Your whole life
is not just this. You do not speak
a language made of this, this is
not your name.

Your name is your own.

Let your name be
The name of someone who
can do the unthinkable:
Stands up and keeps moving.
You are standing. You are taking
a shower and eating breakfast.
You are going to classes
or going to work. You are doing
impossibly hard things. Keep going
and keep going and there
is summer. Laugh even if it is
with rage. Open your mouth
and your fists. Tell the truth.
Tell a friend. Listen to someone
else's heart. It is beating
a miracle. You are
Both here.

When scars are new,
They shine. Be all the glitter
You need.

How To Eat Sugar Cane

THE CRUSH

By Karen Finneyfrock

You stand in a dark room and grow a tree in your chest.
The color pink is your national anthem.
You have fled the burning city, but your pocket smolders.
He bats his eyelids and dust flies.
You are a well trying to quench its own thirst,
a tiger licking its bloody paw.

No eyes are on you, you are all eyes.
He is space age technology.
You are a fist filled with fingers. He is a ghost without a sheet.
You are a buzzing saw in the forest.
The only thing you have ever wanted is more.

REMEMBERING THE NIGHT WE MET

By Cristin O'Keefe Aptowicz

At the after party, you bee-lined right to me,
and I assumed that you were interested in Amanda,
that fluorescent light bulb of a girl, long and thin
and luminous, boys buzzing around her like gnats.

I remember thinking you were clever, buttering up
her geeky friend, the one wearing a dress with sneakers,
the one who kept wandering back to the free food,
the one chomping on a plastic cup filled with ice.

You know: me. So I put my full support behind what
I thought was your project, dutifully introducing you
to Amanda again and again and again, waiting
the requisite two minutes, and then politely exiting

so you could work your magic alone. I remember being
frustrated that you kept coming back to me, wondering,
Does this idiot think I am her pimp or something?
It never occurred to me, I swear, that anyone

would be interested in me, when there were so many
other straightforwardly beautiful options in the room:
girls pink and shiny from wine, their easy smiles,
their straight spines, their clean hair.

When you kissed me at the end of the night, a peck
really, it was enough to pull the whole scene in to clarity.
I didn't know what to say, so I just left, your book
damp in my hand. But know this: you were the U

in my stutter and blush. That one kiss making
the empty O in my chest finally go, *Ohhhh.*

*From Oh, Terrible Youth

For My Childhood Best Friend, Before She Loses Her Virginity In the Balcony of Our High-School Theater When We Are 14: A One Sided Balcony Scene

By Sara Brickman

But soft, what boy's tongue through yonder young mouth breaks;
it is the hissing end, and girlhood is the sun.
Arise, fair anger, and kill the oncoming traffic
of men and boys who in your smile
leave no light for me.

This is how we grow,
the fumbling sex and leaving friends behind.
The knife we must turn to our own names,
just to have boyfriends. The bodies
we will never again know
as sweet in their softness. How
our laughter itself will change
from our own joy to the giggles of impressing our
lovers. O,
would not a rose by any other name
still smell like drug-store nail-polish
and stolen cigarettes? Parting
is such sweet hormonal rage; and they call this *blossoming?*

It was almost like you didn't remember
how we were twin-throated swans,
bedazzling our jean-jackets in the heart
of darkness. How you pushed the boys through
my telephone, like fat peaches. How we swore
we'd never leave each other, that no boy would come
between us. How could we have known love
would rearrange our cells, to want
what would tear us apart?

You are a phantom limb. A star-
crossed animal. My twin swan-neck,
lost in the fog,
calling forever to its mate.

THE WILD DIVINE

By Ada Limón

After we tumbled and fought and tumbled again,
we sat out in the backyard before his parents
came home, flushed and flowered and buzzing
with the quickening ripples of blood growing up.
And I could barely feel my hands, my limbs numbed
from the new touching that seemed unbearably
natural and uncommonly kindled in the body's stove.
Oh my newness! Oh my new obsession: his hands!
I thought I could die and be happy and be humbled
by luck of a first love and a first full-fledged feel.
I wanted to tell my ma. I wanted to make a movie.
I wanted to dynamite out of my bare feet to sky-town,
as we passed the joint in the thick summer's wind
too-rich with oak leaves, eucalyptus, and smoke.
I thought I might have a heart attack: craved
one, wanted the bum-rush of goodbye the way
every kid wants explode when they're finally on fire.
Then, out of the stoned—breath quiet of the hills,
came another animal, a real animal, a wandering
Madrone-skinned horse from the neighbor's garden,
Bowed-back, higher than a man's hat, high up
and hitched to nothing. He rustled down his giant
head where we sat, high and wide-eyed, at this
animal come to greet us in our young afterglow.
He was a horse worthy of complete devotion.
We rubbed his long nose, his large eyes turning
to take us all in, to inhale us, to accept our now-selves.
And he was older, the wise-hoofed big-hearted elder
and I thought, this was what it was to be blessed—
to know a love that was beyond an owning, beyond
the body and its needs, but instead went straight
from wild thing to wild thing, approving of its wildness.

*From Connotation

If My Love For You Were An Animal

By Jennifer L. Knox

It would have three legs left, but only need two.

It would be easy to catch but hard to kill.

It could hold its breath all winter and sleep upside down, anchored under the ice in kelp.

When wet, it would smell like clarinet reeds.

It would break every thing in the house—but purposely, silently, secretly, one item at a time, over hundreds of years, so no one would notice.

Its cry, like an electrical tower wrestling a giant tinfoil dolphin in a meteor crater; its purr, low enough to drive snakes from their dens.

It would be flightless, but you could always find it hiding up high.

Its name would mean magnet. Ants would march towards it over mountains and across the sea floor.

You could elbow it as hard as you wanted to right in the ribs.

It would be so loyal, that if you fell asleep before you took the sleeping pill, it would slip the sleeping pill under your tongue.

*From *No Tell Motel*

THE FIRST
By Shira Erlichman

I would meet her at 6 AM on the front steps of our high school. She would
    be wearing daisy dukes, holding a white bag with two donuts. I would
stare at her crotch while she told me what her parents didn't understand. She would
    pull the blanket over us and flick the movie on. I would
call her little brother "Buddy" and show him a new chord. She would
    date George and Max and coo to me over the phone. I would
spend an entire summer watching her ride her bike away. She would
    stop slicing her thighs, the webbing in between her fingers. I would
spend the night, running my nails through her short maroon hair. She would
    weep snot into my sweatshirt before third period, bleeding. I would
press myself into her locker and talk till the janitors came. She would
    cheer me on, on the field in my blue shorts and CAPTAIN's band. I would
watch her swim in silence, a red needle in the blue. She would
    ace biology while I skipped it to paint, or hide. I would
say Bitch, after hanging up the phone, when she didn't make my birthday. She would
    say Bisexual, and giggle, while in the dark my eyes widened. I would
speak in song lyrics, and write my diary out of pages. She would
    say love first, right before summer Varsity tryouts. I would
leave her house in the early light, blinking, thirsty, without kissing her. She would
    breathe into my ear like a clock, say love first. I would
underestimate my own hands, give up, unspool. We would
    keep it secret for two months like a jar of blood under the bed. We would
tell our mothers, fathers, friends, and some stayed, and some didn't. We would
    bury cats, lose races, argue till sunup. We would
come, hips to mouth, unraveling in laughter, again. We would
    lose us, one cheating with a boy, the other tearing up letters. We would
stop talking, forget, touch, fumble for months our mouths. I would
    scream two years into her soft neck. She would
take up drinking, date men, a girl, erase my number. I would
    study maps, nanny the neighbors' kids, save up. She would
stay in our hometown, work in wildlife, help forests keep from burning.

1943

By Jessica Helen Lopez

It was at 6:15 a.m. when the hospital still slept save
for the squeaking shoes of the white heeled nurses—
the chalk white mistresses of those halls

Dawn had scraped its underbelly across the sky,
cracked the air open like an egg—
the yolk of the sun, tinged blood-spattered pink

You were dying all night. I gasped and you
gasped the hours away, but in the end it was
you dead and me still alive and staring

I watched your silver hair yellow and the nuances
of your skin decay in that instant of death—
watched your five-fingered flower of a hand

how it had
closed and clenched
closed and clenched

Your passing was not unexpected,
we were old and it was your time

At 6:22 a.m. the first fleet of doctors and nurses
entered your room with the usual quiet that
is the hearse that accompanies death

At 6:23 a.m. they flipped the bleeping switches

At 6:24 a.m. they slipped the needles from your closed veins

By 6:30 they led me through the door
and I found myself alone
I held on to my handbag as if it were an anchor

an old woman busy with her sadness

It was then that I remembered
your navy blue bathing suit—

you were so slender and the water
had slipped from your waistline

that day your hair smelled of salt and sea and
the distinct perfection that was you

It was 1943—I was 19 years, 11 months and 25 days
shy of my 20th birthday. You always laughed and said
you were long in the tooth and 6 years my senior,

we both knew that our age difference was not
what forced us to keep a comfortable distance in public
to hide our entwined fingers beneath the beach blanket—
sand pebbles sleeping between our compressed palms

it was the sameness of our silhouette
our mouths that fed each other the language of bleeding
our shared cosmetics, the secret of the pubis
and all the mysteries unlocked when rubbed together

it was the way we combed each other's hair,
washed our feet
me taking hold of your delicate ankle and
swabbing with a wet cloth
your impeccable row of toes

we were roommates
we were childless spinsters
we were condemned by god
and then we passed into
something else unchartered

something else to be regarded
tongue-lashed and branded dykes
by our neighbors

we held fast for sixty-eight years
indefinable, two Helens who had
abandoned their Troy

left the men to squabble over their petty wars

and now at 7 a.m. on a Friday morning,
the world awakens to sip at their mugs of strong coffee
the men wrangle their necks with ties,
the women screw on their faces

we were not quite unrequited love
only unacknowledged

the word wives a foreign pebble on the world's tongue

Oh, how you used to dance
to the Duke's
Sentimental Lady –
a husky saxophone
leaning into the notes like a neck,
my cotton dress pressed
between your cupped palm
and the small of my back

sunshine a gift spilling
through our window

the perfume of us
the perfume of us

You have been fifteen minutes dead
and the doctors surround me
with their clipboards
and questions
and paperwork

Are you kin?
Sisterhood?
Are you kin?

Yes, I say.
One last truthful lie,
my pet

Yes. We are kin.

*From *Malpais Review*

ARE ALL THE BREAK-UPS IN YOUR POEMS REAL?

By Aimee Nezhukumatathil

If by real you mean as real as a shark tooth stuck
in your heel, the wetness of a finished lollipop stick,
the surprise of a thumbtack in your purse—
then *Yes*, every last page is true, every nuance,
bit, and bite. *Wait*. I have made them up—all of them—
and when I say I am married, it means I married
all of them, a whole neighborhood of past loves.
Can you imagine the number of bouquets, how many
slices of cake? Even now, my husbands plan a great meal
for us—one chops up some parsley, one stirs a bubbling pot
on the stove. One changes the baby, and one sleeps
in a fat chair. One flips through the newspaper, another
whistles while he shaves in the shower, and every single
one of them wonders what time I am coming home.

FROM THE ECHO CHAMBER

A Day In the Life of Woman

By Sonya Renee

There will be no bathing today.

Just the cayenne musk of thighs, arm pits

the unmade bed of me;

how creases of belly, fold and wrinkle like laundry,

ignoring the demand that I make myself up.

There will be coffee, the gasoline stain of my teeth,

The whitening the world will ask me to do later.

Computer screens will beg me to shrink, purge,

change to sell you cars and beer,

to sell you parts.

A request to perforate, to better facilitate my shredding.

All this before the dust of sleep

surrenders properly noon. All this,

before I get to name myself.

But name myself I will, with sharp letters,

with tools weighty enough for this planet

constructed of salvaged things. Truth is,

It never mattered what they gave us.

Only what we made out of it. We have always made light.

This planet with so many suns.

So many suns.

13 Ways of Looking at 13

By Patricia Smith

1.

You touch your forefinger to the fat clots in the blood,
then lift its iron stench to look close, searching the globs
of black scarlet for the dimming swirl of dead children.
You thread one thick pad's cottony tail, then the other,
through the little steel guides of the belt. You stand and lift
the contraption, press your thighs close to adjust the bulk,
then bend to pull up coarse white cotton panties bleached blue,
and just to be safe, you pin the bottom of the pad
to the shredding crotch of the Carter's. And then you spritz
the guilty air with the cloying kiss of FDS.
It's time to begin the game of justifying ache,
time to name the mystery prickling riding your skin.
You're convinced the boys can smell you, and they can, they can.

2.

Right now, this Tuesday in July, nothing's headier
than the words *Sheen! Manageable! Bounce!* Squinting into
the smeared mirror, you search your ghetto-ripe head for them,
you probe with greased fingers, spreading paths in the chaos
wide enough for the advertised glimmer to escape,
but your snarls hold tight to their woven dry confounding.
Fevered strands snap under the drag of the wiry brush
and order unfurls, while down the hall mama rotates
the hot comb in a bleary blaze, smacks her joyful gum.
Still, TV bellows its promise. You witness the pink
snap of the perfect neck, hear the impossible vow—
Shampoo with this! Sheen! Bounce! Her cornsilk head is gospel,
it's true. *C'mon chile!* Even mama's summoning burns.

3.

Ms. Stein scribbled a word on the blackboard, said *Who can
pronounce this?*, and the word was *anemone* and from
that moment you first felt the clutter of possible
in your mouth, from the time you stumbled through the rhythm

and she slow-smiled, you suddenly knew you had the right
to be explosive, to sling syllables through back doors,
to make up your own damned words just when you needed them.
All that day, sweet anemone tangled in your teeth,
spurted sugar tongue, led you to the dictionary
where you were assured that it existed, to the cave
of the bathroom where you warbled it in bounce echo,
and, finally convinced you owned that teeny gospel,
you wrote it again and again and again and a--.

4.
Trying hard to turn hips to slivers, sway to stutter,
you walk past the Sinclair station where lanky boys, dust
in their hair, dressed in their uniforms of oil and thud,
rename you pussy with their eyes. They bring sounds shudder
and blue from their throats just for you, serve up the ancient
sonata of skin drum and conch shell, sing suggesting woos
of AM radio, *boom, boom, How you gon' just walk
on by like that?* and suddenly you know why you are
stitched so tight, crammed like a flash bomb into pinafore,
obeying mama's instructions to be a baby
as long as you can. Because it's a man's world and James
Brown is gasoline, the other side of slow zippers.
He is all of it, the pump, pump, the growled *please please please.*

5.
You try to keep your hands off your face, but the white-capped
pimples might harbor evil. It looks like something cursed
is trying to escape your cheeks, your whole soul could be
involved. So you pinch, squeeze and pop, let the smelly snow
splash the mirror, slather your fresh-scarred landscape with creams

that clog and strangle. At night, you look just like someone
obsessed with the moon, its gruff superstitions, its lies.
Your skin is a patchwork of wishing. You scrub and dab
and mask and surround, you bombard, spritz and peel, rubbing
alcohol, flesh-toned Clearasil that pinkens and cakes
while new dirtworms shimmy beneath the pummeled surface
of you. Every time you touch your face, you leave a scar.
Hey, you. Every time you touch your face, you leave a scar.

6.

You want it all: Pickles with peppermint sticks shoved down
their middles, orange-cheesed popcorn mixed with barbecue chips,
waxed lips and werewolf fangs injected with bright blue juice,
red licorice spaghetti whips, pickled pig feet and
ears, hogshead cheese, Lemonheads, grits with sugar, salt pork,
sardines on saltines doused with red spark. All that Dixie
dirt binds, punches your insides flat, re-teaches the blind
beat of your days. Like mama and her mother before
her, you pulse on what is thrown away--gray hog guts stewed
improbable and limp, scrawny chicken necks merely
whispering meat. You will live beyond the naysayers,
your rebellious heart constructed of lard and salt, your
life labored but long. You are built of what should kill you.

7.

Always treat white folks right, her solemn mantra again
and yet again, because they give you things. Like credit,
compliments, passing grades, government jobs, direction,
extra S&H stamps, produce painted to look fresh,
a religion. When the insurance man came, she snapped
herself alive, hurriedly rearranged her warm bulk. He
was balding badly, thatches of brown on a scabbed globe.
Just sign here, he hissed, staring crave into her huge breasts,
pocketing the death cash, money she would pay and pay
and never see again. *C'mere girl, say hello to
Mister Fred.* She had taught you to bow. She taught him
to ignore the gesture, to lock his watering eyes
to yours and lick his dry lips with a thick, coated tongue.

8.

In the bathroom of the what-not joint on the way to
school, you get rid of the starch and billowed lace, barrettes
taming unraveling braids, white knee socks and sensible
hues. From a plastic bag, you take out electric blue
eye shadow, platforms with silver-glittered heels, neon
fishnets and a blouse that doesn't so much button as
suggest shut. The transformation takes five minutes, and you
emerge feeling like a budding lady but looking,
in retrospect, like a blind streetwalker bursting from
a cocoon. This is what television does, turns your

mother into clueless backdrop, fills your pressed head with
the probability of thrum. Your body becomes
just not yours anymore. It's a dumb little marquee.

9.
With your bedroom door closed, you are skyscraper bouffant,
peach foundation, eyelashes like upturned claws. You are
exuding ice, pinched all over by earrings, you are
too much of woman for this room. The audience has
one chest, a single shared chance to gasp. They shudder, heave,
waiting for you to open your mouth and break their hearts.
Taking the stage, you become an S, pour ache into your
hip swings, tsk tsk as the front row collapses. *Damn, they*
want you. You lift the microphone, something illegal
comes out of you, a sound like titties and oil. Mama
flings the door open with a church version of your name.
Then you are pimpled, sexless, ashed and doubledutch knees.
You are spindles. You are singing into a hairbrush.

10.
This is what everyone else is doing: skating in
soul circles, skinning shins, tongue-kissing in the coat room,
skimming alleys for Chicago rats, failing English, Math,
crushing curfew, lying about yesterday and age,
slipping Woolworth's bounty into an inside pocket,
sprouting breasts. Here is what everyone else is doing:
sampling the hotness of hootch, grinding under blue light,
getting turned around in the subway, flinging all them
curse words, inhaling a quick supper before supper
fried up in hot Crisco and granulated sugar,
sneaking out through open windows when the night goes dark,
calling mamas bitches under their breath, staying up
till dawn to see what hides. What you are doing: Reading.

11.
You are never too old. And you are never too world,
too almost grown, you are never correct, no matter
how many times you are corrected. It is never
too late, never too early to be told to cross the
street to the place where the wild stuff is, to suffer her
instructions: *No, not that little switch, get the big one,*

the one that makes that good whipping sound when the breeze blows,
and you are never too fast crossing the boulevard
to bring it back while winged sedans carve jazz on your path.
You climb the stairs, she screams *Get up here!* The door to where
you live with her flies open. She snatches the thorned branch,
whips it a hundred times across the backs of your legs.
You want her to die. Not once, no. Many times. Gently.

12.
That boy does not see you. He sees through you, past your tone
of undecided earth. You are the exact shade of
the failed paper bag test, the Aunt Esther, you are hair
forever turning back in the direction from which
it came. You are clacking knees and nails bitten to blood.
Stumbling forth in black, Jesus-prescribed shoes, you have no
knowledge of his knowledge of hip sling and thrust. That boy
does not see you. So squeeze your eyes shut and imagine
your mouth touching the swell of his forearm. Imagine
just your name's first syllable in the sugared well of
his throat. Dream of all the ways he is not walking past
you again, turning his eyes to the place where you are,
where you're standing, where you shake, where you pray, where you aren't.

13.
You're almost 14. And you think you're ready to push
beyond the brutal wisdoms of the 1 and the 3,
but some nagging crave in you doesn't want to let go.
You suspect that you will never be this unfinished,
all Hail Mary and precipice, stuttering sashay,
fuses in your swollen chest suddenly lit, spitting,
and you'll need to give your hips a name for what they did
while you weren't there. You'll miss the pervasive fever that
signals bloom, the sore lessons of jumprope in your calves.
This is last year your father is allowed to touch
you. Sighing, you push Barbie's perfect body through the
thick dust of a top shelf. There her prideful heart thunders.
She has hardened you well. She has taught you everything.

*From Shoulda Been Jimi Savannah

A POEM FOR MY BREASTS

By Jessica Helen Lopez

The striations are present. The puckered zipper scars like trolley tracks. The brown nipples my daughter never suckled. One small cherry mark on the left tit that I name Blood Star and an assortment of punctuated moles, heavy with the lack of touch. Notice how our areolas sleep like nesting snail, warm mollusk body cupped by bra. I wish this were a love letter or a Nerudaesque ode but you are thirty years of slanted rain. I write this braless, without blouse and warmed by the dapple of white sun bleaching the skin.

No, I lie to you breasts. I sit twisted as always into this vise grip of black satin, underwire sneering. The padding, the lift, the lace and trellis of the pinched breasts. This embarrassingly expensive bra. Understand that I hoped for you before I knew what you were. In my embryo sleep of dark matter and inner space, my phantasmagoric fever, I sought you. First for my mother's, and her already having cut them from her chest, there was nothing left for me.

And then for my own to rise like swelling tides, like a labored moon and tethered star. I courted the both of you. With the wistful mirror gazes of adolescence. The kneading of the tart nipple, the pull, the stretch of skin. The bemoaning vigilance that my body should open into symphony at last.

And in the anger of spit I lashed at you. I despised you like a father.

When you finally rose like a dusty bread know that I never treated you as a spring break calamity. When you sat dripping with unused milk I mourned. When you slept dreamless I let you rest. When you became hardened soured apples I let you live. When you drooped like eyelids I let you be photographed. When you pushed against another woman's body I let you sing. When you agreed to take a husband I vowed we should always be free.

To my first fleshly children who grew despite me, I owe you something holy, reverent. I owe you an apology.

THE WAITING ROOM OF THE GYN

By Cristin O'Keefe Aptowicz

is always filled with babies and pregnant women.
This makes perfect sense, yet I forget every time.
It's like being in a renaissance painting: all stages
of fertility and life, and me, in my unwashed
pants trying to figure out at the best way to say,
Please prescribe to me your cheapest birth control,
without sounding like the failure I sometimes
feel. In the private examination room, I begin
undressing before the nurse has even left.
Oh, and here's your privacy curtain, she says,
pulling it over to separate us without making
eye contact. Ten minutes later, the fingers
of a woman I just met reach around inside of me
as we both try to make small talk. *Everything*
looks to be okay, she says, with a snap of her glove.
Walking out, I always want to be given a hundred
high fives, this annual pilgrimage I loathe but
make. The babies tumble around the waiting room,
in carriages, on the floor, in impossibly large
bellies. One lady is breast feeding when her baby
pulls down the blanket covering them. The woman's
breast is round and full and veined. She apologizes
and replaces it immediately. The women all shake
their heads. *It's all right, honey,* they say, smiling,
Don't worry. We are all women here.

*From *The Year Of No Mistakes*

First Blood After

By Franny Choi

hallelujah. the sheets
are stained with *not*.

organs have exhaled their verdict
and here in the sliding weight of morning, it
starts to seep

away. now
the last threat of a family
darkens softly behind my hip bones.
now i begin the washing and the learning
to be new. now i try
not to wait for him
to come home.

★From *Flicker and Spark*

ECLIPSE
By Aimee Nezhukumatathil

for Pascal

She's been warned not to sleep with moonlight
on her face or she will be taken from her house.

She wears eel-skin to protect herself. She tilts
her face to the night sky when no one is looking.

During the eclipse, eels bubble in their dark

and secret caves. Toads frenzy in pastures
just outside of town, surrounding the dumb cows

in a wet mess of croak and sizzle. Years later,
she would touch the hand of a green-eyed man
by the weird light. Because of him, she plants

a moon garden: freesia, snowdrops, fotherfilla,
bugbane. She is a runner-bean, stretching best

and brilliant in this light. Their child is moon-faced.
She is crazy about them. She is lunatic. She
is taken. She is a hymn book flipped open.

COUNT

By Rachel McKibbens

I lost a lot of blood
the morning I became
a mother. The mirrors spoke
of a seventeen-year old girl
who'd become the amnesia of color.
I was so pale I could walk through walls.

What an astonishing language,
that of a mothering body;
the once kind heart gone
wicked and feral.

Did I tell you, as I nursed my son
that first hour, I felt my bones
begin to thicken, spinning themselves
into a coven of ax handles?

*From *Mammoth*

Aubade With a Broken Neck

By Traci Brimhall

The first night you don't come home
summer rains shake the clematis.
I bury the dead moth I found in our bed,
scratch up a rutabaga and eat it rough
with dirt. The dog finds me and presents
between his gentle teeth a twitching
nightjar. In her panic, she sings
in his mouth. He gives me her pain
like a gift, and I take it. I hear
the cries of her young, greedy with need,
expecting her return, but I don't let her go
until I get into the house. I read
the auspices—the way she flutters against
the wallpaper's moldy roses means
all can be lost. How she skims the ceiling
means a storm approaches. You should see
her in the beginnings of her fear, rushing
at the starless window, her body a dart,
her body the arrow of longing, aimed,
as all desperate things are, to crash
not into the object of desire,
but into the darkness behind it.

BLOODLINE

ON LIVING

By Aracelis Girmay

> *What to do with this knowledge*
> *that our living is not guaranteed?*

What could she do? What does one do
when the mother's mouth is gone;
when the mother closes her eye, the door,
but shuts Girl, this time, out—

Girl wanted words,
but there was only sadness
for the big & dreadful death.

What could she do
but swallow loss?

The black & tumbleweed of those nights
became her home beside her sister.
They mother each other, still, like wolves, like any animal
will do, does, once she's found she's been pushed or fallen
out of the grave, to live.

They live. There is nothing left
to do   but live.

★From *Kingdom Animalia*

DEAR MOM
By Fatimah Asghar

Dear Mom,

I know you're probably on some clouds, or maybe you're eternally
burning somewhere or something. I know that cancer in your boob
wasn't your fault. I know your hair fell out. I know, suddenly, shit
hit the fan, and you didn't have much time. And I know, when it
came down to it, you still thought that you would leave behind our dad.

But when you got pregnant with me, you KNEW you were going
to die. That was a choice you made. You thought, baby or medicine.
And you chose baby. I thank you for that. If I'm ever pregnant I'll try
to do the same. Can't promise I will though. I like being alone.

I mean, I love people too. Sometimes, I feel all the love pouring
from their mouths like headlights and I feel frozen. A world of spotlights
and then I can't move. So, I have to love people from afar. I blame that on you.

What I can't understand is why you couldn't even write a letter.
You knew you were dying. You knew you had three girls that
would have to grow up without you. You see, my dad, I'm not mad
at him for leaving. He didn't know he was going die. Those doctors,
they killed him. It just happened. At least I got memories of him.

You're a picture. People have to point you out to me. "Look babe,
that's your mom. That's your mom." Do you know that? I could
walk by you on the street and I wouldn't know. Do you get that?
Everyone wants to tell me how you were good person. Everyone builds
you of words, of stories. All light: no talk of shadows. At a certain point,
I realized that couldn't be true. No human is as good as what they
say. None. A myth, I built of you. A fucking myth. What good is that?

I don't have anger. Only empty. When I see a picture of you, I feel
nothing. Do you understand that? When people talk about their
parents, about their moms, all the lights in my body turn off. I become a
lightless thing, frozen, in a world of headlighted moving people.

To my Daughter,

I got your letter. It came on the back of the wind.
I know I am far away from you. My days are not

the same as yours. I live mostly in a world of sound.
There are birds chirping. I hear the turtles crawl.

I imagine that I must be near water. This, I feel,
is where you go to walk when your mind needs a rest.

I imagine, this is the place you have allowed me to live.
You built this for me. I know you would never let me burn.

My baby, I am sorry for your empty. I am sorry
for when all the lights turn off. I wish it wasn't so.

I know what it is like to build a world out of pictures,
to want the inside of your eyelids, your own dark walls.

My baby, I am so sorry. Words are not the currency I choose.
That is your money. That is where you build your house.

I, I build mine along water. Along a fluid current.
Now, my love, I no longer know the boundaries of my own body.

I could've written you a thousand letters. None would have set sail.
There are no masts big enough for a dying mother to cast

to a freshly born daughter.

MOTHER IN GREY SCALE

By Denise Jolly

On the mantel sits
A picture frame
It holds my mother
When she was an open fist

Her smile a biblical verse
It does not hold the graveyard
Of my father's fists

They are lonely boxers now
Fighting
His ghost tongue

It is a hallow promise
She remains
A summit of hearts

THE TOOTH FAIRY

By Dorianne Laux

They brushed a quarter with glue
and glitter, slipped in on bare
feet, and without waking me
painted rows of delicate gold
footprints on my sheets with a love
so quiet, I still can't hear it.

My mother must have been
a beauty then, sitting
at the kitchen table with him,
a warm breeze lifting her
embroidered curtains, waiting
for me to fall asleep.

It's harder to believe
the years that followed, the palms
curled into fists, a floor
of broken dishes, her chainsmoking
through long silences, him
punching holes in his walls.

I can still remember her print
dresses, his checkered Taxi, the day
I found her in the closet
with a paring knife, the night
he kicked my sister in the ribs.

He lives alone in Oregon now, dying
of a rare bone disease.
His face stippled gray, his ankles
clotted beneath wool socks.

She's a nurse on the graveyard shift,
Comes home mornings and calls me,
Drinks her dark beer and goes to bed.

And I still wonder how they did it, slipped
that quarter under my pillow, made those
perfect footprints...

Whenever I visit her, I ask again.
"I don't know," she says, rocking, closing
her eyes. "We were as surprised as you."

*From *Awake*

DEEPER THAN DIRT

By Rachel McKibbens

after the poet asked how I would bury my brother

Beyond the carrots and blind white worms, beyond
the yellowing bone orchards and corkscrew roots,
beyond the center of this churchless earth, beloved Peter,
my little sorcerer, brought up dirty & wrong, you deserve more
than to be smothered in mud. For all the gravel you were fed,
for every bruise and knot that named you, I must plant you
in a bed of blood-hot muscle, must deliver you into me, so I may
carry you as the only mother you have ever known.

*From *The Academy of American Poets*

A FAITH LIKE YOURS

By Mayda Del Valle

abuela our common thread began in my mama's womb
spun my fetus like a record in her cipher
sampled your stubborn and mixed in her father's posture
our connection is full circle
abuela you bearer of children
you seer of spirits
you are truly miraculous
you are the whispers of litanies and white lace tablecloths
your melody is captured
in the spilled candle wax of my skin

my tongue's a broken needle scratching through the grooves of a lost wisdom

trying to find a faith that beats like yours
what secrets do your bones hold?
what pattern does your dust settle into
when I beat these drums inside my ribs ?
what color was the soil of your grandmother's garden ?

abuela
how did you pray?
did you store the memory of your creator
in strands of hair tucked into scented soap boxes
or placentas buried under avocado trees?
what reservoir did you pull your faith from?
was it anything like this gumbo
this sancocho
this remix
of rituals and chants sampled
from muscle memory and spirits that visit
my dreams that I struggle to stir into discipline
to honor the unseen
with these shells   this sage   these rudraksha and rosary beads
these white candles   crystals   statues
this sweet water   honey   rum
and sweetgrass

abuela
how did you pray before someone told you who your god should be?
how did you hold the earth in your hands and thank her for its fecundity?
did the sea wash away your sadness?
how did you humble yourself before your architect?
did your lower yourself to your knees
or rock to the rhythm of ocean waves like I do?

abuela
how did you pray?

some say faith is for the weak or small minded
but I search for your faith everywhere
need it to reassemble myself whole
from these shards of Chicago ice and island breezes
so I can rewrite the songs
of your silence and pain
your lonely fists
broken toothed smile
and burdens
into a medley of mantras

wish
you could have shown me its shape
but I know it is here
in every sacred breath
in the shadows of trees you visit me in
in the flicker of flames I stare into searching for what's divine

and I know my body is the instrument my maker uses
to rearrange the broken chords of your history into a new symphony
for my unborn children's feet to dance to

and I see you grandmother
gathering with your sistren
to chant the names of the living and the dead
and remind us all
that whether gathered in a marble temple
around a midnight fire

or block party speakers
we have always raised our hands to the sky
trying to touch the invisible force
that holds these cells together into a fragile mass
children of different nations
but the same vibration
we be sound to beat to bass to bone to flesh
we be sound to beat to bass to bone to flesh
we are all truly miraculous

THE FIDELITY OF CALENDARS

By *Marty McConnell*

in the year of bad but necessary decisions
a boy I would later love yelled at me
for getting into the back of a pickup truck
driven by strangers with my little sister

in Wisconsin. it wasn't the smartest thing
I'd done to date, but certainly
the most entertaining. in the years
of drinking as the key to domestic tranquility

I tacked discount fabric to the walls
to cover the tangerine the previous tenant
had painted over the textured wallpaper. I went
to work every morning. at night the rats

would run the walls and if he were home
he might throw a shoe against the wall
to make them stop. often he wasn't
home. I'd let them run and run. the night

a black wool dress pressed against
the windows. we slept with the windows open
because we couldn't control the heat
in the years of constant overdraft, in the years

of mouths in stairwells, in the years of erupting
bookshelves and faces dissolving in acid
and powder my body grew a spongy,
undeliberate heart. my hands hung useless

at the ends of shrugging arms.
in the year of choosing love
over reason, I paid a stranger
to catalogue my stories while I cried

and blamed my parents. I lived above an alley
in an apartment painted yellow because it received
no natural light. it was my love's
dream home so we lived in it. when she left

I stayed for months, counting the seams
in the concrete ceiling. listening
to the trucks empty the dumpsters
every morning, every morning.

in the year of escape by any means necessary
I recovered my accent. started
believing in ghosts again. calling them
by my grandfather's name. in the year

of escape by any means necessary
again, I remembered my sister's face
as we climbed into the back of the pickup
driven by strangers. the wind on our necks

off the lake, how she hesitated at the tailgate
and looked at me, how she took the boy's hand
and stepped up and in, thinking, as I was, I'm sure of it,
we're together. what's the worst that could happen.

POEM FOR AIMEE ROSE

By April Ranger

Don't step outside—you'll make the stars jealous.

Roy Parker actually said that to my twin sister
when we were sixteen.
I was there. It didn't work.

People fall in love with Aimee Rose
like they are all eight years old,
and she is an ice-cream truck,
and it is always July.

Except October, two-thousand-five
when the guitar player broke her heart
and she dressed up as Miss Havisham
at our literary-themed Halloween party,
and I laughed with her, and cried.

My first memory of us crying together
was when our Mom read the story
of Cain and Abel out loud
and we vowed we'd never kill each other.

Last night I woke her up on the couch
so she'd go to bed,
she rolled over and whispered,
Don't ever die, April.
I said, *Of course I'm going to die.*
I just hope it's before you.

Because I am much more selfish
than Aimee Rose. If we were
a gender-stereotyped old couple,
she'd be the capable woman
telling jokes at my wake,
but I'd be the feeble man
mumbling her name over and over
like it was the only word I ever learned
after we lost the language
we taught each other in the womb.

She hates it when I talk about the womb.
Once we watched the fireworks on Pemaquid Beach,
and a meteor shower occurred simultaneously
in the great large sky
behind our dazzling Prometheus tricks here on earth
and after the last explosion
everyone packed up their blankets and coolers,
but Aimee Rose and I
dug our toes in the cold sand
and watched the falling stars die,
and we didn't make wishes,
we simply witnessed them falling
and held each other's hands-
until the shower ended,
leaving the sky so still and silent,
and we curled together in the bed at my grandmother's,
our warm stomachs rising and falling
while the world went living and dying around us.

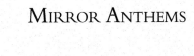

MIRROR ANTHEMS

THE FIDELITY OF SEEKING

By Marty McConnell

at the Des Plaines Park District Leisure Center
I am a tap dance champion. we're all supposed
to have the self-esteem, so there's not a contest
or anything, but I'm winning. never mind

the kids who say that tap is ballet's dumb
cousin, the girls in their tutus swaying like
skinny geraniums, never mind that I was in
ballet until the teacher called me out

for tap, saying ballet was not really my
thing, I can also sing. I'm an excellent
reader. the girls in their pink little slippers
can barely spell *pirouette*. they always

leave out the second t -- it's an easy mistake.
we're dancing to *Raindrops Keep Fallin'
on My Head*. it's a good song for tap,
Nancy says. she lets us call her

by her first name. she also teaches
ballet. she teaches all the dance classes
at the Leisure Center in Des Plaines.
there's a playground here, but it's more

for babies. I do like the swings
though. anyway, my favorite
is the *shuff-le ball change*.
I'm really good at it, Nancy says.

at the recital, we're not supposed
to sing. just tap. Nancy does the dance
in the wings and the other girls keep
looking over to see what she's doing.

I don't. my dad's out there. he ran
a marathon when I was five
and some Saturdays
he lets me go to meetings

and staple newsletters
for his running club
or hand out water if there's
a race. Nancy says it's ok

to look over if you lose
your place. I don't. I don't
lose my place. this isn't math.
shuff-le ball change. I make

the turquoise fringe on my leotard
swing. *shuff-le ball change.* this isn't
dodge ball or the playground
or a race. *shuff-le ball change.*

the spotlight is a big eye
on fire. my dad came.
I can almost see him. I'm winning.

ETYMOLOGY OF THE BEAUTY SHOP

By Jamila Woods

The beauty shop is where I learned how hard it is

to ask for what you want
to say what you don't want
to speak up for what is yours

cringecalm \ 'krinj-käm \ n

> [from the Old English *cringan* meaning "to give way, to fall in battle, become bent, curl up" and the Old French *calme* meaning "the heat of the midday sun, a time when everything rests and is still"]

> 1. It is the way you grit your gums
>   and pretend the forest isn't burning
>   when it is

> 2. It is the way you sing to the woodland animals
>   on your scalp, Snow-White-like, i.e.

>> *Shhhhhhh*, little bunnies, that's not fire on your feet!
>> That's just the sound of Disney Magic twinkling!

> 3. The cringecalm is the way you will do anything
>   to avoid being called "tender headed"
>   to be "tender headed" is to be weak
>   to be weak is to be not strong enough to be beautiful
>   to be beautiful is to fall gracefully in battle
>   become bent, curl up, burn
>   in the heat of the midday sun
>   rest, be still

My hairdresser once said I looked
like I was sick, like I had been living
in a hospital because I had not been
to the beauty shop in weeks, and my roots
grew in and she said I looked sick
or bedridden as if I had not looked
in a mirror for months

clawrub \klo-rᴀb\ n

[from the Greek *khele* or "cloven hoof"
and the Scandinavian *rubbe*, "to rub or scrub"]

1. It is the scrape of Miss Beautician's inch long
   acrylic nails against your head skin

2. It is the dancing of curled taloned birds
   across your skull beneath a cool waterfall

3. It is rainy season, the back of your neck rested on the lip
   of the head sink and you could almost fall asleep
   because the clawrub is a lullaby sung by
   pointy-toed horses galloping into the bones
   of your head and you could almost fall asleep
   closing and opening your eyes in daze
   between the salon ceiling, the soft jiggle
   of her brown arm, the faucet running
   the *rubbe*, the *khele*, and the soft clop
   of hooves above your brow

The beauty shop is where I learned how hard it is

to ask for what you want
because I did not ask for a haircut
sometimes and I still got one
I did not ask for a relaxer
sometimes and she said "But
my hands hurt from combing
your ugly is hurting my hands
won't you make this easier on me?"

I had a perm once
and the church ladies said
it was so long
and I should never cut it

I had a perm once
and it rained and I had to go back

I had a perm once
and my boyfriend wondered
if I ever washed it

I had a perm once
and my sister did too
and my grandmother too
and we went to get it done on Tuesdays
and we listened to Jill Scott play
in the shop until we were blow-dried

And I wore it like Dorothy
and I wore it like Aaliyah
and it was beautiful
and it was Black

But then it hurt my hair
so my hair got cut
the church ladies asked why
my boyfriend didn't say anything

And then it killed my hair
and my hair fell out
and I was still beautiful
but for a while I forgot

I had a perm once
and then I cut it off
and my hair is still beautiful
and my hair is not more black

but still black

PRETTY

By Shaney Jean Maney

When I was seven, I wanted nothing more than to be beautiful.
Not beautiful and smart. Or beautiful and powerful.
Just. Beautiful.

A blonde girl-woman with a miniskirt name like Sarahhh or Jennifer.
I wanted child sized high heels, lipstick, and to be mistaken
for a nine-year-old who could be mistaken for a prostitute.

Instead, I was named Shannon—
A name with mouse brown-hair
and wears the wrong sized culottes.

I took cues on beautifuliality from Vanna White and Miss Piggy.
I posed by the refrigerator like Vanna and asked if anyone
would like to buy a vowellive.★ I batted my eyelashes a lot and slowly
and weird-giggled like a fat pig puppet.

In Junior High, when other girls made wearing shorts seem easy,
I spent half an hour before volleyball practice, every day,
curling my hair.

Once, I dropped my curling iron on my leg.
My thin thigh read Revlon for a week.
All because I wanted curly hair for volleyball.
Practice.

On yearbook day, I wished I had contact lenses so I
swept off my glasses in a moment wherein I expected
the world would turn in a collective gasp, *Shannon!*

They would whisper with glamorous voices.
Shannon, we had no idea you were so physically attractive.
We are so unanimously sorry for treating you like booger-mud.
We had no idea how beautiful you would look—

right now, at age eleven, with your growth spurt gut
hanging out and your stretch pants somehow too snug—
without glasses.

Without glasses, you look just like a young Murphy Brown, they would say.
A young, beautiful Murphy Brown, when she isn't wearing glasses.
You could sell long distance plans for Sprint, they would say.

I had read about "big doe eyes," so I widened my eyes ~~attractively~~
aggressively, so the whites of my eyes could see all the way around.
You know that look people get when their pets die suddenly in front of them?

I would look so beautiful if my eyes looked like that but Smiling.

When the yearbooks were distributed, the picture
was so utterly shocking that everyone laughed
until they cried.

Other things I did for beauty:

I wore deodorant on and in places that did not require it.
I tried to camouflage a hole in my black tank top
by drawing on the underneath skin in permanent marker.

Once, when singing along with/pretending to be in
the music video for the song "Manic Monday,"
I pretended to curl my hair with a comb, wrapped it up

good and tight, all the way up to the crown.
The worst part was the awkward, silent drive to the salon.

I dressed as Barbara Bush for an entire day of 6th grade
when I   misunderstood that the Living Autobiography Book Report
was for just the afternoon (and everyone else was "dressing up" in
"everyday clothes").

I frequently wore the same shirts, pants and blazers as my teachers.
I frequently tried to convince my mom to drop me off
at popular girls' birthday parties to which I was not invited.

I safety pinned my shirts to my underwear so they would stay tucked in.
I hung out with teachers during recess because no one else
appreciated the accuracy of my Ross Perot impression.

I stopped accepting credit for every book I read. I tried to stop
finding jokes so funny so no one could make fun of my laugh.

And the thing about it that gets me now,
is that no one was really watching.
All of these major tragedies,
the fauxiest of pas,
no one cared.

It all seemed so public.
So noticeable.
So odd and unacceptable.

An unwatched tragedy isn't a tragedy.
It isn't anything.

ALLIANCE
By Patricia Smith

All I wanted that year was one of those tall blonde
dolls, always pale-named Susie something, a doll
that bolted forward (*"She's magic! She walks! She
looks just like you!"*) when you squeezed her hand
just so, one of those dolls with flat nightmare hair
the color of exploded corn and a dress that glowed
and crinkled and sparked. I wanted a perfect friend
to stumble ahead with, a unyielding plastic to wrestle
and wake against, all I wanted was blue flutter-lashed
eyes flapping little voodoo, I wanted to fall in love
with and be horrified by her, to search her mouth
for a full tongue, to grow to resent her, to grant her
mysticism and fury, to lock her up in my closet and
watch the doorknob all damn night, waiting for that
slow Twilight Zone twist. All I talked was *Susie this,
Susie that,* scrawling her in tortured block-lettered
pleadings with Santa, taking my father by the hand
and leading him past rows and rows of her shelved
at Kresge's. I said I'd never ever ask for anything
else again ever, not knowing that Barbie, just one
aisle over, was sharpening her fashionable talons,
sniffing the air for fresh breasts and menstrual blood.
I wanted, wanted and prayed for something hard
and possible, my fresh mute walking baby woman.

But on Christmas Eve, when I snuck a peek through
my wishing window into the starry, slanted snow
and saw daddy pull a want-shaped box from the trunk
of his Buick, it didn't stun my belief in the annual
gospel of a porky, apple-cheeked Santa. You know,
I wasn't stupid—at eight, I'd already signed on for
the miraculous black art of white men. They danced
in my cereal, sold detergent to my mother, this one
shimmied down tenement chimneys. I knew Santa

was still coming, tugged by huffing reindeer, fooled
again by my wide-eyed vow that I'd been an angel.
This gift came from another place, for another reason.

I folded my little body into the dark, kept watching.
When I glimpsed pink knees and a sunshiny coif
through the box's cellophane front, I thought it was
only right that my father loved hard enough to introduce
Susie to the dim, resigned sigh of his daughter. All that
frosted night, they must have huddled, plastic against
pulse, discussing my sad soft, the out-loud mistakes
in my walking. Actually, only my father spoke. Susie
simply nodded, her stout legs thrumming, a warm
purpose trembling behind her slammed-shut tempera smile.

*From *Shoulda Been Jimi Savannah*

WHAT'S IT'S LIKE FOR A BROWN GIRL
By Jessica Helen Lopez

What it's like for a brown girl with narrow hips
to sail on in without a lick of Spanish
dancing the *meringue* or *salsa* or *un pachanga*
on the tiny goose pimples of her conquered tongue –

and when the sienna burn of the flushed woman
behind the ancient cash register at the local *taqueria*,

(you know the one. Where *Avenida de Cesar* turns into Bridge
right past the Rio Grande and near that *tiendita* owned
by Rose Marie where anyone with five bucks cans buy
good pink spandex without snags)

face like Moctezuma's lover, eyes like Xilonen,
fertility goddess and eater of the good filth asks –

Quieres tu tacos de carne asada con cebolla y cilantro?
Para aqui or para llevar?

you answer with a dead, dumb tongue
I don't know Spanish

What it's like for a brown girl with big feet
to stumble on into the lily-white halls of academia
and to write poems about red men with big fat hands
abortion and how homemade *menudo*
is a cure all for *crudo*

and when the professor with the broad Germanic
cheekbones and wide-set eyes, two blue marbles pushed
into the dough-like paste of her face says without words
and with a glare the color of a gleaming bullet,
"You slam poets you, with all your hip-hop and speaking in
tongues. I hope you choke on all that alliteration."

The envelope in the mail is addressed to Brown Girl.
It reads, "Well, congratulations *Pendeja*. You just paid $45,000
in tuition so the zipper-lipped teacher with the MFA branded
on her ass could tell you that brown girls must use the back door.
Why don't you go back to Chicano Studies where you belong?"

What it's like for a brown girl with slim wrists
a clavicle like a bird, laughter the size of mountains,
trying not to curse as much as she'd like because
sensibilities like hers are not found in libraries,
courthouses, frilly stages with expensive acoustics,
publishable poems and other respectable places
respectable people convene when they are acting respectable.

But ask a brown girl to name her dogma and she
will with a loving tongue paint the night black-blue
gilded salt where she punched holes for stars.

But ask a brown girl how she loves and she
will whistle wind into existence, weave you something
nice and fine for you to wear on a Friday night
she will pluck out every last hair from her head and
cross-stitch like her *abuelita* taught her – she will shimmy
and shake her way into Saturday

But ask a brown girl how to dance and she
will shoot from her hip like a cowgirl Guadalupe,
A Lucky Stripe dangling from her lip and wearing
a cock-sure cap like a bad attitude

What it's like for a brown girl to spread herself
thin like *masa* across two countries, three border towns,
lost languages, imperceptible boundaries and

you brown as dirt
simple as sand
quiet as the unfurling of
the morning leaf
you the crimson dawn

s t r e t c h in g
her arms across the sky

you brown and
soft and saying
all the things
your mother
taught you not
to say

*From *Malpais Review*

FIREFLY

By Sara Brickman

The sound of the locker door slamming
against the empty hall in middle school: hollow.
Hollow, the weight of my hand on the knob of the public library door
where I come every day after school
to do my homework.

This is the library across the street from the McDonald's
where five girls will jump me in the parking lot.
Surround me with their vicious stares,
their nails sharpened, and hair
teased into aerosol fireballs-in-waiting.

These are the girls who have made it their life's work
to hate me. To make sure I never have a place
to sit at lunch. Girls
who have everything: fancy houses and fancy clothes,
and still find that fish-hooking their hoop earrings into me
fills their bellies.

This is the year I get suspended,
when I push the boy who has been taunting me
for weeks and he
punches me in the mouth. The year
I fall asleep every night begging God to turn me *into a dragon,
or a boy,* or
a different kind of girl. One
who understands how to wear these bones
like an expensive outfit.

The sky is cool today.
I have shown up to school in the wrong outfit
again. The packs of girls roam the halls.
They sit together at lunch. Sometimes
I can fool them. Sit quietly for long enough

that one will even talk to me. My solitude
becomes a point of pride, evidence
that *I am better than them* and this makes me
mean. I plot a million kinds of revenge.
I stand in the backyard
and scream for so long I think I might pass out.
All the adults
keep saying how *bright* I am.
When no one will answer my Friday night phone calls,
I go to a movie with my parents.

I want to grow up to be a famous actress,
because no one laughs at famous actresses
when they get food on their shirt.
No one calls famous actresses ugly.
Hideous. Disgusting. Stupid. No one laughs
at famous actresses in their bunk at camp
when they get their period, and bleed the sheets. No one
steals famous actresses shoes
on the class trip to Canada
and makes famous actresses
walk   barefoot
across the parking lot,
                    where there is broken glass.

I am 13. New York
is waiting. The moon is full
and bloodless. Broadway is a mason jar
full of exploding lights, so I grit my teeth
and dream of marquees. Everyone
says I am a bright girl.
Incandescent.

THE AUDITION
By Amber Tamblyn

True story:
Through the scratched glass doors I dance
into a florescent lit lobby with four fold up chairs
occupied by actresses far more famous than me,
and one audition sign in sheet.

I wear a Quinceanera dress with sequins so sinister,
the daylight squints.
Its train is off the rails.
You haven't seen eye-shadow until you've seen
"Rosie The Riveter's Great Grandmother's Mother's Lover No. 6".

I sign myself in as The Great and Powerful.
Announced myself in color.
Glinda the Bad Witch.
Mandy Moore's just not ready.

My tulle spills into the audition room before I do.
I don't make entrances. I make entryways.

I sing for the director like Carly Simon
wrote that song about me.
Like there's blood in the notes
and this room is an emergency transfusion.
I know my lines by heart.
I know my heart, line for line.

I leave the audition room in a plume of perspired glitter.
Mark territory by tossing my chandelier earrings into the mint tray.
I blow a kiss to the water cooler.
Never look back.

If you're gonna go all out, go for broke.
Go for the throat of the thing that chokes.

Have the kind of faith in yourself
that makes your girlfriends *amen*.

Have the kind of love for your body
that teaches others how to love their own.

Even if you don't get the part.
Even if Mandy really *was* ready.

ON WITHDRAWING

By Franny Choi

At times, I am in the habit of taking half a step back into the curtain of my body, as a means of regaining human confidence, by which I mean recharging the energy spent in being seen. The outer surface of my face being the inverse of glow-in-the-dark tape onto which the stage hand pours flashlight fuel backstage before the show. By contrast, my luminescence drains slowly over the course of a day and drinks greedily from the dark, from places under covers, beneath stacks of notebooks, behind the two-way mirror of makeup. When such hideouts are unavailable (for instance, at a long dinner with strangers following a small but tragic mistake), there exists a reserve supply of darkness in the rumbling cave I call my body. The method is this: I draw a circle around myself, the radius extending as far as my glass of water. This becomes the fence around my field of vision and my fingers. I settle into my own nucleus. I burrow. I speak, but the sound is muffled by the walls of limestone and the slow dripping. I am a submarine peeking through the curtains of the waves. I am a stowaway in a suit of armor. I am an eavesdropping cat on the radiator, so much paw to groom. I tell my friends I'm not feeling well, as I plug the opposite of a flashlight into my fuel tank and wait.

BLOOM
By Tara Hardy

Little Sister, beware of the bonnet of needles
that is a traditional life. All you'll see at first
are the pretty horses, the strong steeds
come to rescue you out of the mud. The mud
of circumstance, or worse, the mud of
"Now that feminism has arrived, what am I to do
with all this choice?" This vast landscape begging

for footprint." This is when he'll come riding
up with a worn spot in his saddle that is just
your size. He will have the world in his eyes
and it will be the world you think you're
entering when you slide into the stirrups

of wife. But here's the thing, even if he lets you
ride astride and not side saddle, there will be
duty. There will be the serious end of a mop,
a mother in law, and holidays for which
you may even want to bake. None of these
is, by definition, a bad thing. But for every girl,
there is also a bee teeming under the lovely
hood she wears down the aisle. And the bee

is purpose, the bee is foot print. As soon as we
slip into this world they stand us on a pad of ink
and then a pad of paper. But Little Sister, this is not
the only mark you were ever meant to make.

The question, "What am I to do with my life"
is a brutal God with brutal power to wrestle
out of your hands anything he demands. Because
if you dare to look your own gifts in the eye,
that is if you dare to step to the altar of your widest
possibility, the answer may come back, "Girl,
get off that horse. Pull those pretty pearled
pins he gave you out of your hair and set off
in nothing but a single pair of shoes."

My husband loved my poems, but found poetry
inconvenient. What I mean by this is there were
too many holiday eves upon which I did not bake
a pie, but left him home alone while I went out
to hunt for Haiku. This may have been cruel.
Little Sister, the God, the bee may demand
you develop a capacity for cruelty. Not only
will you be asked to bleed for your purpose,
but you may be asked to bleed the ones you
love. Why do this? On some days I don't

know. On some days the world selfish dances
out of my mirror-mirror onto my morning
toothbrush. But Little Sister, when I dare to look
my own gifts in the eye, when I dare to step
to the altar of my widest possibility, the answer
comes back: I do this, because to not do it is a gown
made of bees. I am so welted without my

purpose. I do this because out here in the wrong
shoes over the next ridge I may find a company
of dancing deities. Goddamn it, I do this
because there are little sisters everywhere
quietly bleeding under their bonnets trying
not to cry out as the wall close in around us.
I do this because I am wild as bees and you
cannot make a pet of me. This I do because
a brutal God gave me a grand gift and the real
selfish would be to withhold it. It's not that I don't

want a prince. More that I have faith that all
the wrong angles of which I'm built will be enough
for he or she who trips over me on his own path.
When that happens, my true prince will not ask me
to dismount my shabby horse or bake consistent
crust. My true prince will not fit me for a bonnet
of needles and ask me to pretend it's love. Because
true love, when I finally accident upon it will find me
most worthy when I am in pursuit of bloom,
clearly already married to my own hive.

THE WILD LANGUAGE OF STARS

Daughter

By Brynn Saito

One day you will find yourself on the sharpest
edge of yourself. If you're lucky

someone will answer the phone and say it's for you
and you'll come inside.

The voice is an open refuge.
Forgiveness is a tower of hands. Once when I was young

I walked through a clock then under a bridge and my whole life was lit
by a camel cigarette. I met a man

who was not your father but he played the jazz piano so we fell in to it
and let it reign. Of course

love is kind. But sometimes a person must pursue a plague
that could do some justice

to the storm within.
You'll see.

You will be thirsty too.
You will stop believing in September.

You will suddenly become aware
of the fact of your heart only when a part of it

goes missing. Well don't believe
what they tell you. No one likes change.

One day you will find yourself resisting your own waking.
Try tending to the sacred
and see where that gets you.
Try rolling through your life like a rusted train through a stockyard nation.

Nothing fills a cup like moonlight. Nothing.
No one will twist you like a man

will twist you, but that's the deal. That's how books
get written. But don't believe

what I've told you. Convince yourself.
Then burn the sage

and claw your way
through every oak on the rotting mountain.

*From *The Palace of Contemplating Departure*

DISCIPLE
By Mindy Nettifee

The best advice I ever got about how to heal
came from a beleaguered camp counselor
who found herself suddenly surrounded
by a flock of heaving sobbing twelve year old girls.
It had been billed as a session on conflict resolution,
an alternative to wood cookie crafts, or horseshoes,
and maybe she should have seen it coming,
how water seeks the cracks in any dam.

One girl had been brutally sexually assaulted
by the preschool director, and had not slept
through the night alone since.
One had been molested by her foster brother,
who sliced his arms with scissors in the bedroom dark.
One had been strangled by her own mother,
who later found God and apologized,
and then punished her for not offering up

the fish and loaves of forgiveness instantly,
the forgiveness which her mother had been promised
by some pastor that she deserved now, and would receive
through the mysterious machines of grace;
the kind that multiplied and magnified and
fed the endless hunger at the center of things.
There were other stories.
Abuse is a word that sounds powerful in your head

and goes limp the moment you speak it,
hanging like a soaked wet curtain
around the things we cannot bear to know.
I don't remember the counselor's name, or
what she looked like, just that she was an enormous
buoy of a woman. That her voice was deep
and calm and quavered at all the right turns.
That she sat in a way that trained gravity.

How unprepared she must have felt,
to see the sharks swimming in our eyes,
to have been handed the heavy anchors
of our trust. What well of strength did she draw from?
What inheritance of bedrock and granite and spine?
What gospel stolen from the bent melted steel of kitchen knives?
She absorbed every blow of every word.
When we had finished, when we were softened

by confession, she took a breath and began.
Without getting into the kind of details that get attention,
she told us the story of her own early ruin,
of the lifetimes of gentle obligation it left in its wake.
The heart and the mind and the body
might never align on the requirements of joy.
The mind must be taught patience with the heart.
The heart must learn faith from the body.

The body must be tended lovingly and unwaveringly, an infant.
The heart will take its own sweet time, and cannot be rushed.
"Just fake it 'till you feel it," she told us,
and like that, gave us permission
to put on the tight masks of adulthood,
to build walls around what was
too tender and shocked;
to survive.

*From *Rise of the Trust Fall*

THE SAVING TREE

By Ada Limón

This is the cooling part of the fever,
when everything: the jumping girder
of the Golden Gate's red limb, the tall
metal tree house of the Empire State,
the black rock cliff on the Sonoma Coast,
the drawer's leftover pills, the careless
cut, the careening car, the cross walk,
the stop/go, the give up, give up, done,
all of it, slows to a real nice drive by. A view
of some tree breathing and the mind's wheels
ease up on the pavement's tug. That tree,
that one willowy thing over there,
can save a life, you know? It saves
by not trying, a leaf like some note
slipped under the locked blue door
(bathtub full, despair's drunk), a small
live letter that says only, *Stay*.

*From *Thrush*.

I Am Not Ready to Die Yet

By Aracelis Girmay

after Joy Harjo

I am not ready to die yet: magnolia tree
going wild outside my kitchen window
& the dog needs a house, &, by the way,
I just met you, my sisters & I
have things to do, & I need
to talk on the phone with my brother. Plant a tree.
& all the things I said I'd get better at.

In other words, I am not ready to die yet
because didn't we say we'd have a picnic
the first hot day, I mean,
the first really, really hot day?
Taqueria. & swim, kin,
& mussel & friend, don't you go, go, no.

Today we saw the dead bird, & stopped for it.
& the airplanes glided above us. & the wind
lifted the dead bird's feathers.

I am not ready to die yet.
I want to live longer knowing that wind
still moves a dead bird's feathers.
Wind doesn't move over & say *That thing*
can't fly. Don't go there. It's dead.
No, it just blows & blows lifting
what it can. I am not ready
to die yet. No.

I want to live longer.
I want to love you longer, say it again,
I want to love you longer
& sing that song
again. & get pummeled by the sea

& come up breathing & hot sun
& those walks & those kids
& hard laugh, clap your hands.
I am not ready to die yet.

Give me more dreams. To taste the fig.
To hear the coyote, closer.
I am not ready to die yet.
But when I go, I'll go knowing
there will be a next time. I want
to be like the cactus fields
I drove through in Arizona.
If I am a cactus, be the cactus
I grow next to, arms up,
every day, let me face you,
every day of my cactus life.
& when I go or you go,
let me see you again somewhere,
or you see me.

Isn't that you, old friend, my love?
you might say, while swimming in some ocean
to the small fish at your ankle.
Or, *Weren't you my sister once?*
I might say to the sad, brown dog who follows me down
the street. Or to the small boy
or old woman or horse eye
or to the tree. *I know I knew I know you, too.*
I'm saying, could this be what makes me stop
in front of *that* dogwood, train whistle, *those* curtains
blowing in that window. See now,
there go some eyes you knew once
riding the legs of another animal,
wearing its blue sky, magnolia,
wearing its bear or fine
or wolf-wolf suit, see,
somewhere in the night a mouth is singing
You remind me   You remind me
& the heart flips over in the dusky sea of its chest

like a fish signaling *Yes, yes it was me!*
&, yes, it was, & you were there, & are here now,
yes, honey, yes hive, yes I will, Jack,
see you again, even if it's a lie, don't
let me know, not yet, not ever, I need to think
I'll see you, oh,
see you
again.

*From *Kingdom Animalia*

OKLAHOMA

By Jan Richman

In the wild and silly West, my mother visited me
from death. We sat on a peeling wooden bench
five feet back from the forever tracks, dust
wearing the land like an old monkey fur, hot
wind slowing down time. Her gloved hands, her
buttoned boots, her pigskin valise. Awnings
that sheltered us from love. The five o'clock train
howled from practically Texas, throwing its
rumble down the smooth metal arms that reached
beyond our feet. Change, change. The body
of noise passed close enough to touch, and you
were in her place. Your grin rode high on your
face. I tell you, I liked you from the very first.
When you kissed me, my mouth could be any shape.
I didn't know sadness from happiness, or how many
limbs we had, wheat stalks waving like mad, or
who was feeding whom. All our disappointments
were on the lam. The sky was the color of sand,
the stretch and tenor of brindled sand. My
bed rocked and woke, my hands tucked in, warm
skin folded my own swells and curves, and taking
in the dawn marks I baby-cried for another room,
wider and incurable, despairing of a tender
ear, a listening womb, a lover west and south,
a railway transfer bending time, a breast
in the mouth.

★From *Because the Brain Can be Talked Into Anything*

THE NUTRIONIST

By Andrea Gibson

The nutritionist said I should eat root vegetables,
said if I could get down thirteen turnips each day
I would be grounded, rooted.

Said my head would not keep flying away to where the darkness lives.

The psychic told me my heart carries too much weight,
said for twenty dollars she'd tell me what to do.
I handed her the twenty and she said, "Stop worrying darling,
you will find a good man soon."

The first psycho-therapist said I should spend three hours a day
sitting in a dark closet with my eyes closed and my ears plugged.
I tried it once but couldn't stop thinking
about how gay it was to be sitting in the closet.

The yogi told me to stretch everything but truth,
said focus on the out breath,

said everyone finds happiness
if they can care more about what they can give
than what they get.

The pharmacist said Klonopin, Lamictil, Lithium, Xanax.

The doctor said an antipsychotic might help me forget
what the trauma said.

The trauma said, "Don't write this poem.

Nobody wants to hear you cry about the grief inside your bones."
But my bones said, "Tyler Clementi dove into the Hudson River
convinced he was entirely alone."

My bones said "Write the poem."
To the lamplight considering the river bed,
to the chandelier of your faith hanging by a thread,
to everyday you cannot get out of bed,
to the bulls eye of your wrist,
to anyone who has ever wanted to die:

I have been told sometimes the most healing thing we can do

is remind ourselves over and over and over
other people feel this too.

The tomorrow that has come and gone
and it has not gotten better.
When you are half finished writing that letter
to your mother that says "I swear to God I tried,
but when I thought I'd hit bottom, it started hitting back."

There is no bruise like the bruise
loneliness kicks into your spine
so let me tell you I know there are days
it looks like the whole world is dancing in the streets
while you break down like the doors of their looted buildings.

You are not alone
in wondering who will be convicted of the crime
of insisting you keep loading your grief
into the chamber of your shame.

You are not weak
just because your heart feels so heavy.
I have never met a heavy heart that wasn't a phone booth
with a red cape inside.

Some people will never understand
the kind of superpower it takes for some people
to just walk outside some days.

I know my smile can look like the gutter of a falling house

but my hands are always holding tight to the rip chord of believing
a life can be rich like the soil,
can make food of decay,
turn wound into highway.

Pick me up in a truck with that bumper sticker that says,
"It is no measure of good health
to be well adjusted to a sick society."

I have never trusted anyone
with the pulled back bow of my spine

the way I trusted ones who come undone at the throat
screaming for their pulses to find the fight to pound.

Four nights before Tyler Clementi
jumped from the George Washington bridge
I was sitting in a hotel room in my own town
calculating exactly what I had to swallow
to keep a bottle of sleeping pills down.

What I know about living
is the pain is never just ours.

Every time I hurt I know the wound is an echo,

so I keep a listening for the moment the grief becomes a window,

when I can see what I couldn't see before
through the glass of my most battered dream
I watched a dandelion lose its mind in the wind

and when it did, it scattered a thousand seeds.

So the next time I tell you how easily I come out of my skin
don't try to put me back in.

Just say, "Here we are" together at the window
aching for it to all get better

but knowing there is a chance
our hearts may have only just skinned their knees,
knowing there is a chance the worst day might still be coming
let me say right now for the record,
I'm still gonna be here
asking this world to dance,

even if it keeps stepping on my holy feet.
You, you stay here with me, okay?
You stay here with me.
Raising your bite against the bitter dark,
your bright longing,
your brilliant fists of loss.

Friend, if the only thing we have to gain in staying is each other,
my god that is plenty
my god that is enough
my god that is so so much for the light to give
each of us at each other's backs

whispering over and over and over,
"Live. Live. Live."

*From *Pole Dancing To Gospel Hymns*

My, My, My, My, My

By Tara Hardy

Take that thing that happened. To you.
Open it like a concealed rose. Hold it up
to the nose of someone else. Let them
tell you that you still smell sweet. So

sweet. Let that person who loves you pluck
petals out of the gully of your wound. Let
her shave them into points and sail them
back into your heart like paper airplanes. For

that fist at the center of your pulse is of what
you have always been made, despite
your fingers being tipped in thorn. Use them
now to shred the sheets. Shred the night.

No one needs to sleep under that much
cover or on that much polite. Slit the sky.
Let the Gods fall out. The ones who could've
let that thing happen in the first place.

Catch them in your pockets. Catch them
in your chest. Put the God back
in your chest, God after God after God. Until
you know yourself. Again. Repeat.

Take that rose, the one your flesh wounds
around. Open it and open it and open it.
Toss bits of your scar into the air
like goddamned wedding rice. Or bird seed.

Let some of them sprout. Into so much green
green new day it makes your shins hurt
with how much you want to run. Forward.
And meet the world without all those

red whorls, those old scars, those stuck stitches in your side. And we, we will marvel at your silhouette. My, we'll say. My, my, my, my, my! Doesn't she run like an un-flowering?

GIRL WITH RED BICYCLE

By Gypsee Yo (Jonida Beqo)

The girl with the red limping bicycle
and scraped knees and hands wipes
tears with the hem of her dress, sore alone.

By now she knows boys
will always push her out
of the way, rather than lose
to a girl who is good at everything.

Boys, brothers, cousins, and friends
immune to the spell of blooming flowers
on summer frocks, unimpressed
with quick tongue and wit, tell her
the likes of her all die alone.

No man would chain his heart to hers,
an anchor diving too deep to rescue.

The strap of her torn sandal,
unstitched like her pride, tugs her
ankle by the reins on the long way
home, that humbling walk across hot
pavement soft as bruised flesh.

Across the rooster yard of boyhood cacophony
the bicycle chain drags on the ground like a white flag.

But she squeezes her fists until knuckle-white
hands become walls her pride can lean on.

Let them sweat trying to catch
my hair in the wind. I will ride.

I don't care if their feet never leave the shore.
I will always dive, headfirst and unafraid.

No matter how deep the anchor plunges
I will always rescue myself.

GET MORE COURAGE

To read more about the authors in this anthology,
read interviews, watch videos, and find more poems,
please visit www.courageanthology.com

Author Bios

 **Chrstin O'Keefe Aptowicz** is the author of five books of poetry (_Dear Future Boyfriend_, _Hot Teen Slut,Working Class Represent_, _Oh, Terrible Youth and Everything is Everything_) as well as the nonfiction book, _Words In Your Face: Guided Tour Through Twenty Years of the New York City Poetry Slam_. Cristin's most recent awards include the ArtsEdge Writer-In-Residency at the University of Pennsylvania (2010-2011), a National Endowment for the Arts Fellowship in Poetry (2011) and the Amy Clampitt Residency (2013). Her sixth book of poetry, _The Year of No Mistakes_, was released by Write Bloody Publishing in Fall 2013 and her second nonfiction book, _Curiosity: Thomas Dent Mutter and the Dawn of Modern Medicine_, will be released by Gotham Books (Penguin) in Fall 2014.

 **Fatimah Asghar** is an award-winning poet and performer who is almost always in-between two places. Her literary work hovers between prose and poetry, examining fact through a lyrical lens. She has won numerous awards for experimental risk-taking in her work, which has appeared in Muzzle Magazine, DecomP, Fringe Magazine, and many others. In 2011 she created Bosnia and Herzegovina's first Spoken Word Poetry group, REFLEKS, while on a Fulbright studying theater in post-genocidal countries. Last year she was a Multicultural Fellow at the Steppenwolf Theater, where she worked in the Literary department. She is the co-founder of The Glass City Project, a Chicago-based arts organization that combines poetry, theory, and activism.

Sara Brickman is an author, activist, and the 2011 Seattle Women of the World Poetry Slam Champion. Her work has been published or is forthcoming *and Bestiary Magazine, Hoarse, and The New.* A 2012 Artist Trust EDGE fellow, Sara has taught workshops in poetry, performance, and creative non-fiction at the Bent Writing Institute, Richard Hugo House, and as a mentor with Youth Speaks Seattle. She has performed her work at venues across North America, including the Bumbershoot Music Festival, Northwest Folklife, and as a speaker at Texdx Seattle. IN 2010 she founded a multimedia performance series in her living room called The Hootenanny, to showcase groundbreaking writers and musicians. She lives and works in Seattle, WA, where she would love doing the robot with us.

Traci Brimhall is the author of *Our Lady of the Ruins* (W.W. Norton), selected by Carolyn Forché for the 2011 Barnard Women Poets Prize, and *Rookery* (Southern Illinois University Press), selected by Michelle Boisseau for the 2009 Crab Orchard Series in Poetry First Book Award. She has also written two poetry comic books, *How to Write a Love Poem* and *The Wrong Side of Rapture*, with illustrator Eryn Cruft. Her poems have appeared in *The New Yorker, Slate, Ploughshares, The Believer, The New Republic,* and *Best American Poetry 2013.* She received the 2008-2009 Jay C. and Ruth Halls Poetry Fellow at the Wisconsin Institute for Creative Writing, the 2012 Summer Poet-in-Residence at the University of Mississippi, and a 2013 Fellowship in Literature from the National Endowment for the Arts.

Franny Choi is a Korean-American poet, playwright, and fiction writer. A Pushcart Prize nominee and award-winning performer, she has been invited to read at schools, festivals, and performance venues across the country. She has been a finalist at the three largest adult slam competitions in the nation, and her literary work has appeared in *Fringe, Apogee, Tandem, Issues,* and others. Her play *Mask Dances* was staged in the 2011 Writing is Live Festival at Rites and Reason Theatre. Franny's first full-length collection of poems is forthcoming on Write Bloody Publishing.

Mayda Del Valle has been described by the Chicago Sun Times as having "a way with words. Sometimes they seem to flutter and roll off her lips. Other times they burst forth like a comet streaking across a nighttime sky." A proud native of the South Side of Chicago, she has appeared on 6 episodes of Russell Simmons Def Poetry Jam on HBO and was a contributing writer and original cast member of the Tony Award winning Def Poetry Jam on Broadway. She also toured with Norman Lear's Declare Yourself Spoken Word Tour , a non-profit, non-partisan project created to encourage young voter registration for the 2004 presidential elections. Smithsonian Magazine chose her as one of "America's Young Innovators in the Arts and Sciences" and Oprah's O Magazine named her as one of 20 women for the first ever "O Power List."

Shira Erlichman is a nationally acclaimed poet, musician, and artist. A Pushcart Prize nominee who has toured the country with some of the nation's leading performers and writers, her prolific and unique style has brought her acclaim as "one of the most original and compelling voices in performance poetry." Her award-winning music has appeared in multiple independent films and has been featured on NPR. She has shared stages with Ani Difranco, TuNe-YaRds, Coco Rosie, and Mirah. She has been independently recording and releasing her records for over 10 years. Originally from Brookline MA, she now lives in Brooklyn NY in an indoor treehouse.

Erica Miriam Fabri is a poet, performer and photographer. Her book of poems, "Dialect of a Skirt" was a finalist for the Paterson Poetry Prize and was included on the list: Best Books of 2009 at About.com as well as the Poetry Foundation's bestseller list for October 2010. She wrote, directed and starred in the short film "The Baxter Street Blues" which was based on her poem by the same name and was an official selection for the New York City Independent Film Festival in 2013. She teaches writing & performance workshops at various colleges & universities in New York City, including Pace University, New York University, Columbia University and The City University of New York (CUNY). She also runs the Creatively College Bound program for the hip-hop and poetry-based non-profit organization, Urban Word NYC.

Karen Finneyfrock is the author of two young adult novels, *The Sweet Revenge of Celia Door,* and, *Starbird Murphy and the World Outside,* both published by Viking Children's Books. Her second book of poems, *Ceremony for the Choking Ghost,* was released on Write Bloody press. She is a former Writer-in-Residence at Richard Hugo House in Seattle and teaches for Seattle Arts and Lectures' Writers-in-the-Schools program. In 2010, Karen traveled to Nepal as a Cultural Envoy through the US Department of State to perform and teach poetry and in 2011, she did a reading tour in Germany sponsored by the US Embassy.

Andrea Gibson is not gentle with her truths. It is this raw fearlessness that has led her to the forefront of the spoken word movement– the first winner of the Women's World Poetry Slam – Gibson has headlined prestigious performance venues coast to coast with powerful readings on war, class, gender, bullying, white privilege, sexuality, love, and spirituality. Her work has been featured on the BBC, Air America, C-SPAN, Free Speech TV and in 2010 was read by a state representative in lieu of morning prayer at the Utah State Legislature.

Aracelis Girmay is originally from Santa Ana, California and currently lives in New York. She is the author of *Teeth* and *Kingdom Animalia* as well as the collage-based picture book *changing, changing.* She teaches at Hampshire College in the School for Interdisciplinary Arts.

Daphne Gottlieb stitches together the ivory tower and the gutter just using her tongue. She is the author and editor of nine books, most recently the poetry book *15 Ways to Stay Alive* as well as co-editor (with Lisa Kester) of *Dear Dawn: Aileen Wuornos in her Own Words.?* She is the editor of *Fucking Daphne: Mostly True Stories and Fictions* and *Homewrecker: An Adultery Reader*, as well as the author of the poetry books *Kissing Dead Girls, Final Girl, Why Things Burn* and *Pelt*, and as the graphic novel *Jokes and the Unconscious* with artist Diane DiMassa. Gottlieb has also appeared across the country with the Slam America bus tour and with notorious all-girl wordsters Sister Spit. She has performed at festivals coast-to-coast, including South by Southwest, Bumbershoot, and Ladyfest Bay Area.

Tara Hardy is the working class, queer, chronically ill, Femme poet who founded Bent, a writing institute for LGBTIQ people in Seattle. She is the author of *Bring Down the Chandeliers*, by Write Bloody Press, a former Seattle Poet Populist and writer in residence at Richard Hugo House. She is an alumnae of Hedgebrook and holds an MFA from Vermont college. Tara tours as a poet, performer, and teaching artist.

Denise Jolly is the former Executive Director of Youth Speaks Seattle Youth Speaks, co-host and facilitator of the Seattle Poetry Slam, Poetry Curator for The Round a live multidisciplinary collaborative arts show, and Vice President of Stronghold Productions, an organization that worked collaboratively to build large scale, fully sensory kinetic sculptures. In 2013 she ranked 5th in the Women of the World Poetry Slam, was the 2009 San Francisco

Grand Slam Champion and member of the 2009 San Francisco Slam team who ranked 3rd in the nation. Denise has taught and performed at colleges, universities, community centers, public and private schools all over the US. She likes doing great things with amazing people and being moved by art, community and how the two work together.

Sarah Kay is a poet from New York City who has been performing her spoken word poetry since she was fourteen years old. She is perhaps best known for her talk at the 2011 TED conference, which garnered two standing ovations and has been seen over three million times online. Sarah holds a Masters Degree in The Art of Teaching from Brown University and an Honorary Doctorate in Humane Letters from Grinnell College. Her first book, "B" was ranked #1 Poetry Book on Amazon. Her second book, "No Matter the Wreckage" is available from Write Bloody Publishing. Sarah is the founder of Project VOICE, an organization that uses spoken word poetry to encourage people to engage in creative self-expression in schools and communities around the world.

Jennifer L. Knox's new book of poems, *The Mystery of the Hidden Driveway*, is available from Bloof Books. Her other books, *Drunk by Noon* and *A Gringo Like Me*, are also available through Bloof. Her poems have appeared four times in the *Best American Poetry* series (1997, 2003, 2006, and 2011) as well as the anthologies *Great American Prose Poems, From Poet to Present* and *Best American Erotic Poems*. Her work has also appeared in publications such as *The New Yorker, American Poetry Review, Fence, McSweeney's,* and *Bomb*. She is currently at work on her first novel.

Dorianne Laux the recipient of two Best American Poetry Prizes, a Pushcart Prize, two fellowships from The National Endowment for the Arts and a Guggenheim Fellowship. Widely anthologized, her work has appeared in the Best of APR, The Norton Anthology of Contemporary Poetry and The Best of the Net. In 2001, she was invited by late poet laureate Stanley Kunitz to read at the Library of Congress. Laux has been teaching poetry in private and public venues since 1990 and since 2004 at Pacific University's Low-Residency MFA Program. In the summers she teaches at the Esalen Institute in Big Sur, California and Truro Center for the Arts at Castle Hill. She and her husband, poet Joseph Millar, moved to Raleigh in 2008 where she teaches poetry in the MFA program at North Carolina State University.

Ada Limón is the author of three collections of poetry, *Sharks in the Rivers, This Big Fake World,* and *Lucky Wreck.* Her work has appeared in numerous magazines and journals including, Harvard Review, TriQuarterly Online, Poetry Daily, and The New Yorker. She has received fellowships from the Provincetown Fine Arts Work Center, the New York Foundation for the Arts, and won the Chicago Literary Award for Poetry. She served as a judge for the 2013 National Book Award in Poetry and will join the 2014 faculty for the low-residency MFA-Latin America for Queens University of Charlotte. She is currently finishing her first novel, a book of essays, and a fourth collection of poems. She works as a writer and lives in Kentucky and California.

Jessica Helen Lopez is a nationally recognized award-winning poetry slam champion, and holds the title of 2012 Women of the World (WOW) City of ABQ Champion. She's also a member of the Macondo Foundation. Founded by Sandra Cisneros, it is an association of socially engaged writers united to advance creativity, foster generosity, and honor community. Her first collection of poetry, Always Messing With Them Boys (West End Press, 2011) made the Southwest Book of the Year reading list and was also awarded the Zia Book Award presented by NM Women Press. She is the founder of *La Palabra* – The Word is a Woman collective created for and by women and gender-identified women. Lopez is Ted Talk speaker alumni and her talk is entitled, Spoken Word Poetry that Tells HERstory.

Shanny Jean Maney wakes up at 5AM every day to teach English at a laboratory high school that teaches teachers how to teach. She co-founded the literary phenomenon The Encyclopedia Show, which aims to trick writers and audiences into exploring the underexplored. Her first full-length book of poems, of which she is very proud, is available from Write Bloody Publishing and is titled *I Love Science!*.

Marty McConnell is the author of *wine for a shotgun* (EM Press, 2012.) A member of seven National Poetry Slam teams representing New York City and Chicago, she is the 2012 National Underground Poetry Individual Competition (NUPIC) Champion. McConnell transplanted herself from Chicago to New York City in 1999, after completing the first of three national tours with the Morrigan, an all-female performance poetry troupe she co-founded.

She received her MFA in creative writing/ poetry from Sarah Lawrence College, and for nearly a decade, co-curated the flagship reading series of the New York City-based louderARTS Project. She appeared twice on HBO's *Def Poetry Jam*.

Rachel McKibbens is a poet, activist, playwright, essayist and is a New York Foundation for the Arts poetry fellow and author of the critically acclaimed volume of poetry, *Pink Elephant* (Cypher Books, 2009) and *Into the Dark & Emptying Field* (Small Doggies, 2013). She is a nine-time National Poetry Slam team member, has appeared on eight NPS final stages, coached the New York louderARTS poetry slam team to three consecutive final stage appearances, is the 2009 Women of the World Poetry Slam champion and the 2011 National Underground Poetry Slam individual champion. For four years McKibbens taught poetry through the Healing Arts Program at Bellevue Hospital in Manhattan and continues to teach poetry and creative writing and give lectures across the country as an advocate for mental illness, gender-equality and victims of violence and domestic abuse.

Mindy Nettifee is an award-winning writer and performance poet and co-founder and Director of the Write Now Poetry Society. She is the author of two full-length collections of poetry, *Sleepyhead Assassins* (Moon Tide Press) and *Rise of the Trust Fall* (Write Bloody Press), and the collection of essays on writing, *Glitter In The Blood* (Write Bloody Press). She has taught and performed at over 200 schools, theatres and community centers and has produced unique literary events for the last decade for the

Smithsonian Project, the Getty Center, the Los Angeles County Arts Commission and others.

Aimee Nezhukumatathil is the author of three award-winning collections of poetry: *Lucky Fish, At the Drive-In Volcano,* and *Miracle Fruit.* Her honors include the Pushcart Prize and a poetry fellowship from the National Endowment for the Arts. She is professor of English at SUNY-Fredonia where she received a Chancellor's Medal of Excellence and lives in western New York with her husband and their two young sons.

April Ranger's poems have appeared or are forthcoming in *Muzzle Magazine, apt,* and *Off The Coast.* She is the author of three chapbooks: *We Are Not As Strong, The Sacred Heartbeat of Consent,* and *Blood Oranges, Top Bunk.* A long-time member of Boston's poetry community, April represented Boston Cantab at the National Poetry Slam in 2008, 2010 and 2011. She competed at two Individual World Poetry Slams as the Boston representative, and has toured extensively across the United States. April's first full-length play, *Streetsweepers,* won the Nicole Dufresne Playwriting award while she studied theatre at Emerson College. Her plays *Frabjous Day* and *Those Still Living* were produced at the Boston Theatre Marathon in 2008 and 2010.

Sonya Renee Taylor is a Performance Poet, Activist and transformational leader and is a National and International award winning writer and performer, published author, and global change maker. She has shared her work and activism across the US, New Zealand, Australia, England, Scotland, Sweden, Canada and the Netherlands. She is the founder and CEO of The Body is Not An Apology, an international movement of radical self-love and body empowerment that reaches over 100,000 people weekly. weekly. Sonya has been seen, heard and read on HBO, BET, MTV, TV One, NPR, PBS, CNN, Oxygen Network, New York Magazine, MSNBC.com, Today.com, Huffington Post, Vogue Australia, Shape.com, Ms. Magazine and many more. She has shared stages with such luminaries as Hillary Rodham Clinton, Harry Belafonte, Dr. Cornell West, Amiri Baraka and more.

Jan Richman is the author of *Thrill-Bent*, a picaresque novel about roller coasters, Tourette's syndrome, and the peccadilloes of an armchair thrill-seeker (Tupelo Press, 2013). She received the Walt Whitman Award from the Academy of American Poets for her poetry collection *Because the Brain Can Be Talked Into Anything* (LSU Press, 1995), an NEA grant in Literature, and a Masters from New York University. She lives in San Francisco, California, and is working on a(nother) semi-autobiographical novel.

Brynn Saito is the author of *The Palace of Contemplating Departure*, winner of the Benjamin Saltman Poetry Award from Red Hen Press (2013). She also co-authored, with Traci Brimhall, *Bright Power, Dark Peace*, a chapbook of poetry from Diode Editions (2013). Brynn's work has been anthologized by Helen Vendler and Ishmael Reed; it has also appeared in *Virginia Quarterly Review*, *Ninth Letter*, *Hayden's Ferry Review*, and *Pleiades*.

Patricia Smith is the author of six books of poetry, including Blood Dazzler, a finalist for the National Book Award, and her latest, Shoulda Been Jimi Savannah, winner of the Phyllis Wheatley Award and finalist for the William Carlos Williams Award from the Poetry Society of America and the Balcones Prize. She is a 2012 fellow at both the MacDowell Colony and Yaddo, a two-time Pushcart Prize winner and a four-time individual champion of the National Poetry Slam, the most successful poet in the competition's history. Patricia is a professor at the College of Staten Island and an instructor in the MFA program at Sierra Nevada College, where she is currently serving at Distinguished Visiting Professor in the Humanities. She is married to Bruce DeSilva, the Edgar Award-winning author of the Liam Mulligan crime novels.

Amber Tamblyn is a Venice, California native. She has been a writer and actress since the age of 9. She has been nominated for an Emmy, Golden Globe and Independent Spirit Award for her work in television and film. Currently she stars as the salty, alcoholic, womanizing Jenny Harper on CBS', "Two and a Half Men". She has published two collections of poetry, *Free Stallion* (Simon & Schuster 2005) and *Bang Ditto* (Manic D. Press 2009). She co-founded the nonprofit, Write Now Poetry Society (writenowpoets.org) and has a poetry review column in Bust Magazine. Her forthcoming third book of poetry, *Dark Sparkler* (Harper Collins 2015) is an intimate look at the lives and deaths of child star actresses with accompanying art by such artists as David Lynch and Marilyn Manson. She lives in Brooklyn.

Jeanann Verlee is an author, performance poet, editor, and former punk rocker. She is author of Racing Hummingbirds (Write Bloody Publishing), which earned the Independent Publisher Book Award Silver Medal in Poetry. Verlee is also winner of the Sandy Crimmins National Prize for Poetry. Her work appears in a number of journals, including The New York Quarterly, Rattle, and failbetter, among others. She is former director of Urbana Poetry Slam, and has represented New York City ten times under both NYC-Urbana and NYC-louderARTS at the National Poetry Slam, Individual World Poetry Slam, and Women of the World Poetry Slam. Verlee lives in New York City with her husband and a pair of origami lovebirds. She believes in you.

Holis Wong-Wear is a writer, performer & creative producer. She is one-third of The Flavr Blue, one-half of hip-hop duo Canary Sing, provides the vocals for acoustic R&B outfit The Heartfelts, and is featured on "White Walls" by Macklemore & Ryan Lewis. She is the Operations Director for Blue Scholars and is currently a teaching artist with Youth Speaks Seattle.

Jamila Woods is a poet, singer, playwright, and teaching artist from Chicago, IL. A Pushcart Prize nominee, her poetry has been published in a variety of journals, including *MUZZLE* and *Radius*. Jamila was named Best Female Poet (CUPSI) in 2009, and is the two-time winner of the Louder Than A Bomb College Slam (2008 & 2010). She is a founding member of Young Chicago Author's Teaching Artist Corps, where she teaches poetry writing & performance at high schools throughout Chicagoland. Her first chapbook was released in 2012 by *New School*

Poetics Press. In 2011, Jamila became the frontwoman of soul-duo band Milo&Otis. Their first album The Joy, was hailed as "mold-shattering" by the *Washington Post.*

Gypsee Yo (Jonida Beqo) is a native of Albania, currently residing in Atlanta, GA. She is a performance artist whose work aims to blur the lines between genres. Her background includes successful projects in theatre, dance, storytelling, and performance poetry. She is the regional Southern Queen of Slam (2008), Atlanta's Slam Champion (2006 – 2009) and a three time National Poetry Slam semi-finalist (2006 – 2008). She has ranked two times as first runner up in the Women of the World Poetry Slam in Detroit, MI (2009), and Columbus, OH (2011). Her three poetry collections in Albanian *I Do Not Fit Inside my Body*(1998), *The Last Nail* (1999), and *When Life Grows Roots Inside a Suitcase* (2003) are critically acclaimed titles.

Notes & Acknowledgements

Thank you to the editors and publishers of the journals, magazines and books in which the following poems first appeared:

"Estephania" and "Remembering the Night We Met" by Cristin O'Keefe Aptowicz appeared in *Oh, Terrible Youth*, Write Bloody Press.

"The Waiting Room of the GYN" By Cristin O'Keefe Aptowicz appeared in *The Year Of No Mistakes*, Write Bloody Press.

"Shoulda Been Jimi Savannah" and "13 Ways of Looking at 13" and

"Alliance" by Patricia Smith all appeared in *Shoulda Been Jimi Savannah*, Coffee House Press.

"I Sing the Body Electric, Especially When My Power's Out" and

"A Letter to the Playground Bully, From Andrea, Age 8 ½" by Andrea Gibson appeared in *The Madness Vase*, Write Bloody Press.

"The Nutrionist" by Andrea Gibson appeared in *Pole Dancing To Gospel Hymns*, Write Bloody Press.

"13" By Aracelis Girmay appeared in *Teeth*, Curbstone Press.

"On Living" and "I Am Not Ready to Die Yet" by Aracelis Girmay appeared in *Kingdom Animalia*, BOA Editions.

"7 Things I Never Told My Older Sister, Because I know Better, In Reverse Chronological Order" by Mindy Nettifee appeared in *Sleepyhead Assassins*, Moon Tide Press.

"Disciple" by Mindy Nettifee appeared in *Rise of The Trust Fall*, Write Bloody Press

"Swarm" by Jeanann Verlee appeared in *Racing Hummingbirds*, Write Bloody Press.

"The Wild Divine" by Ada Limón appeared in *Connotation*.

"The Saving Tree" by Ada Limón appeared in *Thrush*.

"If My Love For You Were An Animal" by Jennifer L. Knox appeared in *No Tell Motel*.

"1943" and "What's it's like for a Brown Girl" by Jessica Helen Lopez appeared in *Malpais Review*.

"First Blood After" by Franny Choi appeared in *Flicker and Spark*.

"The Tooth Fairy" by Dorianne Laux appeared in *Awake*, BOA Editions.

"Daughter" by Brynn Saito appeared in *The Palace of Contemplating Departure*, Red Hen Press.

"Oklahoma" by Jan Richman appeared in Because the *Brain Can be Talked Into Anything*, Louisiana State University Press.

"Count" by Rachel McKibbens appeared in *Mammoth*, Organic Weapon Arts.

"Deeper than Dirt" by Rachel McKibbens appeared in *The Academy of American Poets*.

This anthology owes an incredible debt to so many people and poems and forces of inspiration, but specific thanks must go out to all the contributors for their talent and strength; Claire Williams and Julia Seldin for their dedicated assistance; the sisterhood of writers at Pink Door for their encouragement and advice; the board of directors at Write Now Poetry Society for their time and support; and the incredible team at Write Bloody, led by Derrick Brown, for their hard work and steadfast belief in the transformative power of poetry. Finally, Karen Finneyfrock, Mindy Nettifee and Rachel McKibbens would like to thank you, for reading this book, and passing it on.

IF YOU LIKED THIS ANTHOLOGY, YOU'RE GOING TO LOVE . . .

Write About An Empty Birdcage
Elaina M. Ellis

The Smell of Good Mud
Lauren Zuniga

After the Witch Hunt
Megan Falley

New Shoes on a Dead Horse
Sierra DeMulder

Good Grief
Stevie Edwards

Learn Then Burn
Tim Stafford and Derrick Brown

Write Bloody Publishing distributes and promotes great books of fiction, poetry, and art every year. We are an independent press dedicated to quality literature and book design, with an office in Austin, TX.

Our employees are authors and artists, so we call ourselves a family. Our design team comes from all over America: modern painters, photographers, and rock album designers create book covers we're proud to be judged by.

We publish and promote 8 to 12 tour-savvy authors per year. We are grass-roots, D.I.Y., bootstrap believers. Pull up a good book and join the family. Support independent authors, artists, and presses.

**Want to know more about Write Bloody books, authors, and events?
Join our mailing list at**

www.writebloody.com

Write Bloody Books

CPSIA information can be obtained
at www.ICGtesting.com
Printed in the USA
FSOW03n0942080617
34862FS